A Live The

GW01003489

CLEAR WHITE LIGHT

Written by **Paul Sirett**
Inspired by the songs of **Alan Hull**
and *The Fall of the House of Usher* by Edgar Allan Poe

First performed at Live Theatre on
Tuesday 23 October 2018

This play is dedicated to the memory of Alan Hull.
It is also dedicated to everyone who has ever had to face a struggle
with their mental health and all the incredible women and men
who have worked in NHS Mental Health services over the
past seventy years. Thank you.

Location: St. Nicholas's Hospital, Gosforth
Time: November 2015

CAST

Charlie Hardwick	MADDIE, A woman in her 50s
Joe Caffrey	ROD, A staff nurse in his 50s
Bryony Corrigan	ALISON, A student nurse in her early 20s
Phil Adèle	AARON, Male patient / DOCTOR
Alice Blundell	JO, Female nurse
Dale Jewitt	CHARLIE, Male patient
Billy Mitchell	BARRY, Male patient
Ray Laidlaw	PERCUSSION

CREATIVE TEAM

Directed by	**Joe Douglas**
Designed by	**Neil Warmington**
Dramaturgy by	**Max Roberts**
Musical Direction and performed live by	**Ray Laidlaw & Billy Mitchell**
Lighting Design by	**Ali Hunter**
Sound Design by	**Dave Flynn**
Production Manager	**Drummond Orr**
Stage Manager	**Craig Davidson**
Deputy Stage Manager	**Heather Robertson**
Costume Supervision	**Lou Duffy**
Creative Producer	**Graeme Thompson**
Technician	**Craig Spence**
Casting Directors	**Lucy Jenkins CDG & Sooki McShane CDG**
Set Build	**Durham Scenic Workshops**
National PR	**Chloe Nelkin Consulting**
Lead Image Design	**Michael Cranston**

Thanks

The family of Alan Hull, staff at St. Nicholas Hospital, staff at Recovery College Collective, Siobhan Chadwick, John Salkeld, Shaun Gowens, Gez Casey, Clare Overton, Mike Brown, Paul Aziz, Alison Mountain, Dan Seale, Jane Holman, Pete Peverley, Phil Corbitt, Chris Connel, Jude Nelson, Jackie Edward, Brian Lonsdale, John Lawlor, Northumberland Tyne and Wear NHS Foundation Trust, Dr Melanie Waters, Northumbria University and NCJMedia Photo Archives.

Max Roberts reflects on his journey, and that of the development of the play, *Clear White Light*

I first came to Newcastle in the early of Autumn of 1973 to study drama at what was then Northern Counties College on Coach Lane in Benton (now part of Northumbria University). To my mind Tyneside seemed an attractive place – a long way from home and the beginning of a new chapter in my life.

The band *Lindisfarne* were part of that early experience – their music seemed distinctive and representative of the new culture I had begun to inhabit. The opening song in *Clear White Light* epitomises that:

> 'I can see it all now falling into place, we can leave all our troubles behind. You can tell at a glance by the look on my face that it's really whippin' up my mind.
>
> And It'll be alright we'll have a drink on a Friday Night. It'll be oh so good, we'll do everything that I know we should.'

But it wasn't just good time rock 'n' roll music, the songs were lyrical and political; they contained a pride of place and a distinctive sound that fused 70's rock, blues and traditional influences with a lyrical content clearly influenced by Guthrie, Dylan and The Beatles.

Alan Hull, the leading songwriter of the group, whose songs have inspired this play was one of the most talented and original songwriters of his generation, nationally and internationally, but a Geordie through and through.

In my ambition to become involved in theatre I was lucky enough to be taught and inspired by a fantastic playwright called C.P. Taylor. Later Tom Hadaway and Alan Plater shaped my sensibility and vision as a director of plays and I was privileged to be able to develop my craft and direct shows by all three of those brilliant writers.

What those guys taught me was to find out about the place that I was living and working in. Its history, its culture, its politics, its landscape, its literature and to keep abreast of the issues and concerns that effect its people.

As the Artistic Director of Live Theatre, Newcastle upon Tyne, I needed to harness the above into a policy and a mission. I soon realised that if I was going to succeed in achieving my aims I was only ever going be as good as the writers, actors and artists I worked with. Theatre is a truly collaborative process.

I eventually managed to activate a vision that sought out talented writers who shared my sensibility and who wanted to write about the constituency Live Theatre serves. A new generation of writers following in the slipstream of Cecil, Tom and Alan's prodigious talent came through, along with a wave of actors, artists and arts administrators who helped the theatre to thrive and flourish.

Memorable plays came into being by fine writers including Lee Hall, Julia Darling, Pater Straughan, Paul Sirett, Shelagh Stephenson, Michael Chaplin, Sean O'Brien, David Almond, Paddy Campbell, Patrick Marber and most recently DC Jackson and Alex Oates

Clear White Light has been 'in development' for several years. I was lucky enough to work once with Alan Hull before his untimely death, but have known Ray Laidlaw for some considerable time, and I'm now delighted that our joint ambition to create a play with Alan's music has come to be. Ray and I wanted to find a vehicle for Alan's songs that would not only interest fans of our generation but a new and younger audience who would enjoy discovering the music for the first time.

Paul Sirett was the writer who has made it happen. We had collaborated successfully in the past and Paul has a real skill in creating theatre that harnesses popular music. A chance meeting where we discovered a shared love of the music of *Lindisfarne* finally triggered the project. Paul's undertaken several drafts and we had a few false starts along the way – but we kept going back to Alan's music and then Paul remembered a story Ray had told us about 'the early years' of the band and a quote he uncovered by Alan.

'We are all on the brink of drowning in a sea of madness'

Many of his songs are about society's outsiders, the dispossessed and oppressed. There are songs about love, loneliness, regret and depression and others are angry anthems of injustice. And of course, there are quirky and funny ones inspired by the culture of Alan's beloved Tyneside.

Before Alan joined up with Ray, Simon Cowe, Rod Clements and Ray Jackson to form *Lindisfarne*, Alan worked as a mental health nurse at St. Nicholas Hospital in Gosforth; by his own admission he wasn't the best nurse in the world, but he played the piano and sang songs with the patients and Ray said he let the old fellas keep their socks on when they went to bed, which they appreciated. I suppose we might call all that 'therapy' today. He also read Edgar Allan Poe stories on the long night shifts. A Poe story *The Fall of the House of Usher* struck a chord and inspired the song *Lady Eleanor*. And when returning home one day after a shift he played his wife the embryonic version of a song that gives the show its title *Clear White Light*.

Thus, the premise for the play came to fruition. We certainly didn't want to create a 'jukebox' musical stringing together the 'hits songs' but rather create a contemporary drama that explored issues around mental health and caring in an accessible manner where the songs and Alan's lyrics became an integral part of the narrative.

I thought it was an appropriate gesture to offer up the direction of the play to our new Artistic Director Joe Douglas and he was delighted to take it on as his first production for the company. That was quite a wrench, but it just seemed the right thing to do. Seeing and hearing the words, action and songs blend together as the play slowly and rather magically comes to life has been uplifting, quite emotional in fact and I can't wait to see it up and running in front of a packed audience.

I'm thrilled that two established Live Theatre actors (Joe Caffrey and Charlie Hardwick) are back on our stage joined by Bryony Corrigan and Phil Adèle, Alice Blundell and Dale Jewitt – three young, super talented actor/musicians from the region. They'll be playing alongside Ray Laidlaw and another *Lindisfarne* member Billy Mitchell who jointly undertake the musical direction of the show. Watching Ray and Billy work with the company – especially the younger actor/musicians – has been a joy to behold and I know our audience are in for a real musical treat.

I am looking forward to another 'special' night out in a very 'special' theatre; Live Theatre, Newcastle upon Tyne.

Max Roberts, Emeritus Artistic Director, Live Theatre

Max Roberts has recently stepped down as Live Theatre's Artistic Director. The Board of Directors have appointed him as Emeritus Artistic Director, supporting Live Theatre's new Artistic Director, Joe Douglas. Max will carry on directing plays and has several in development with some of our audience's favourite writers and new and emerging talents who are also under commission.

Alan Hull, St. Nick's Hospital and *Clear White Light*

Alan Hull was already an accomplished songwriter and performer when he took a job in the late 1960s as a trainee psychiatric nurse at St. Nicholas's Hospital in Newcastle. He originally took the job out of necessity but his experiences with the patients had a major effect on his thinking and consequently his songwriting. Alan was fascinated by human behaviour and the protocols that decide what is 'normal'. St. Nick's gave him ample opportunity to observe and he composed many of what became his classic songs whilst working there. Alan was also an avid reader and was heavily into the work of Edgar Alan Poe. He read *The Fall of the House of Usher* during this period, sometimes during quiet periods on night-shift. Alan observed and learned from the patients and discovered that some of the most disturbed could be easily pacified by him simply playing the piano or letting them keep their socks on in bed. Following his experiences at St. Nick's Alan questioned traditional definitions of sanity. He often said that sanity is an illusion, there are only degrees of insanity.

I was aware of Alan from around 1964 when I watched him perform with his then group *The Chosen Few*. They did rather well, they had records out, played in Hamburg and had their own radio show. Following the demise of *The 'Few* Alan was in and out of groups and by the late 1960s he was having a stab at a solo career. I first began making music with him in 1969 and was astonished by not only the number of songs he had written, but also his gift for memorable melodies and thought-provoking lyrics. He was truly world class...and he was right here amongst us on Tyneside. When Alan joined *Lindisfarne* it was a no-brainer, he found the sympathetic musicians he had been looking for and we gained a formidable front-man and composer that perfectly complemented the music we were already making. He was, and always will be, the most gifted songwriter I have ever shared a stage with.

Alan was always searching for new challenges as a songwriter, he was visibly elated when he finished a new song or recording. The last time I spoke to him was in November 1995 when he was nearing the completion of his *Statues and Liberties* album and he was buzzing with the excitement of it all. Unfortunately he didn't live to see the universally positive reviews that followed its commercial release.

Clear White Light is inspired by Alan's short but intense time as a psychiatric nurse. The play places some of his songs into an exciting and contemporary drama with themes that as a lifelong socialist, Alan would certainly recognise. Hopefully the play will throw a light on his influences while also introducing his wonderful music to a new audience. I think he would have loved it.

Ray Laidlaw, *Lindisfarne*,
Musical Director and performer

CAST

Charlie Hardwick

Charlie first worked at Live Theatre in 1988 in Michael Chaplin's *Hair In The Gate* and subsequently appeared in over twenty productions including *Cabaret, Bandits, Two, Seafarers, Close The Coalhouse Door, Your Home In The West, Buffalo Girls* and lastly, in 2002, Sean O'Brien and Julia Darling's *Double Lives*.

Charlie recently played Peggy White in Sting's musical *The Last Ship*, and has performed in a ream of plays for Northern Stage and companies around the country including Lee Hall's *Cooking With Elvis* and *The Awkward Squad* in the West End, and *Hyem* (Theatre503). She is best known for playing Val Pollard in ITV's *Emmerdale* for over a decade, winning awards for Best Comedy Performance, Best On-Screen Performance, Best Partnership and Best Episode for her exit.

Her film credits include *Purely Belter* (FilmFour), *Billy Elliot* (BBC Films) and *The Scar* (Amber Films), for which she won best actress at Monte Carlo Film and TV Awards. Her TV credits include *Byker Grove, Our Friends In The North, EastEnders, Casualty* (all BBC), *The Royal, See You Friday,* and Catherine Cookson's *Tide Of Life* and *Colour Blind* (all ITV) and *Different For Girls* (Jackdaw). Charlie also sings with Newcastle's brilliant band of women *Kissed*.

Joe Caffrey

Joe trained at LAMDA. His theatre credits include *The Last Ship* (Northern Stage/UK Tour), *St George and the Dragon* (National Theatre), *The Girls* (West End), *Iris* (Live Theatre) *Light Shining In Buckinghamshire* (National Theatre), *Cooking with Elvis* (Live Theatre/West End/Tour), *Wet House*

(Live Theatre/Soho Theatre), *The Pitmen Painters* (Live Theatre/ National Theatre/West End/Tour), *A Walk On Part* (Live Theatre/ West End), *Much Ado About Nothing*, *The Globe Mysteries*, *Loves Labours Lost* and *We the People* (Shakespeare's Globe), *Billy Elliot The Musical* (West End) and *Keepers of the Flame* (RSC/ Live Theatre).

His television and film credits include *Wolfblood*, *Clay*, *Doctors*, *Holby City*, *Badger*, *Spender*, *Hetty Wainthrope Investigates*, *Attachments*, Byker Grove and *Ain't Misbehavin'* (all BBC), *The Bill*, *Heartbeat*, *Distant Shores*, *Catherine Cookson's Colour Blind*, *Quayside*, *Waiters*, *The Last Musketeer* and *Soldier, Soldier* (all ITV). Films include *In Fading Light* (Amber Films), *The One and Only* (Assassin Films), *Bridget Jones – The Edge of Reason* (Working Title Films) and *Victoria and Abdul* (BBC Films).

Bryony Corrigan

Bryony trained at LAMDA and is a member of Mischief Theatre Company.

She recently appeared at Live Theatre in *My Romantic History*. Her other theatre credits include *Mischief Movie Night* (Arts Theatre/ UK Tour), *The Play That Goes Wrong* (Broadway/West End), *Peter Pan Goes Wrong* (West End), *How I Learned to Drive* (Southwark Playhouse) and *Lights! Camera! Improvise!* (West End/Trafalgar Studios/Arcola Theatre/Edinburgh Fringe).

Her television credits include *Good Omens* (BBC), *A Christmas Carol Goes Wrong* (BBC), *Peter Pan Goes Wrong* (BBC), *Inspector George Gently* (BBC), *Holby City* (BBC), *Downton Abbey* (ITV) and radio *Christmas Goes Wrong* (BBC Radio).

She has appeared in short films *Tiny Bible*, *Four-Sight* and the video games *Squadron 42* (Cloud Imperium Games) and *Dark Souls 3* (Bandai Namco Entertainment).

Phil Adèle

Phil is a Teesside-born, London-based actor-musician.

Prior to appearing in *Clear White Light*, Phil has also appeared in *Little Shop Of Horrors* (UK Tour), *Handbagged* (English Theatre Frankfurt), *The Invisible Man* (Queen's Theatre Hornchurch), *Wind In The Willows* (Sixteen Feet Productions), *The History Boys* (Theatre By The Lake) as well as an episode of *Red Dwarf* (Dave), several short films, high profile commercials and other projects.

Phil is excited to be heading back to the North East to work on this exciting new piece and to work with Live Theatre for the first time.

Alice Blundell

Alice trained at ALRA and is co-founder of The Letter Room Theatre Company.

Alice's theatre credits include *Alice in Wonderland*, *James & the Giant Peach*, *Wizard of Oz*, *The Christmas Grump* and *Tallest Tales from the Furthest Forest* (Northern Stage), *Beyond the End of the Road* (November Club), *This World Here... Nomhlaba Le* (Curious Monkey), *Far From the Madding Crowd* (Watermill, Newbury), *Treasure Island* (Queens Theatre Hornchurch) and *No Miracles Here*, *Five Feet in Front* and *Bonenkai* (The Letter Room).

Her television credits include *Hospital People* (BBC) and *Inspector George Gently* (BBC).

Alice is thrilled to be making her first appearance at Live Theatre in *Clear White Light*.

Dale Jewitt

Dale trained at the University of Northumbria and North at Northern Stage.

He has previously appeared at Live Theatre in *10 Minutes to... Make a Memory* and *Mixtape 90s*. His other theatre credits include *Romeo and Juliet*, *The Taming of the Shrew* and *Much Ado About Nothing* (all with Theatre Space North East), *Manifesto for a New City* and *Animal Farm* (Northern Stage), *Dr Mullins Anatomy of the Theatre Royal* and *Teacups, Zebra and Dancing Kaisers* (November Club), *Rainbird* and *The Dirty Flea-Bitten Scrounging Bastard* (Cloud Nine Theatre Company), *The Wind Road Boys* (Enter CIC), *Snow White* (Mendes Management) and *Puddles Adventure* and *The Cow Jumped Over the Moon* (The Customs House, South Shields).

Ray Laidlaw (Musical Director & Percussion)

Ray was born in Tynemouth and started playing in groups at fourteen. He was educated in Newcastle, mostly at the legendary Club A'Gogo. The group he started with some mates in 1966 changed their name to *Lindisfarne* in 1970. They then became very popular and had lots of hit records.

He was interested in making music films and met TV director Geoff Wonfor and together they produced and directed *Lindisfarne*'s early promotional films.

He's continued to combine performing, TV and video production, event production and the administration of the *Sunday for Sammy Trust*.

Billy Mitchell (Musical Director, Musician, Actor)
Billy founded the seminal group *Jack the Lad* in the 1970s, who were musically deft and wondrous, and also un-hinged. He spent half a lifetime with Maxie Peters as the wonderfully wacky *Maxie and Mitch*, then eight years as front man of the legendary *Lindisfarne*.

In 2005 he recorded *The Devils Ground*, and in one enthusiastic review of the album, was noted as *'one of the finest singers on the planet.'* He recently performed with *Roger Daltrey* of *The Who*, *Paul Weller*, *Jools Holland*, *Mark Knopler*, *Sting*, and *Brian Johnson* of *AC/DC* at Sage Gateshead.

Billy has recently been touring with *Lindisfarne* pal, drummer Ray Laidlaw, with *The Lindisfarne Story*, a show documenting the history of the North East's favourite band, in songs, stories and visuals.

CREATIVE TEAM

Paul Sirett, Writer

Paul is a playwright, dramaturg and musician.

As a playwright, Paul has over twenty productions to his name including *Lush Life* at Live Theatre and two West End transfers, *Rat Pack Confidential* and *The Big Life* for which he was nominated for an Olivier Award. Recent productions include *Oxy and the Morons* (New Wolsey Theatre) and *Reasons to be Cheerful* (Graeae).

As a dramaturg, Paul has worked on numerous productions for companies including the RSC, Soho Theatre and the Ambassador Theatre Group. Most recently, Paul adapted *The Who's Tommy* for D/deaf and disabled actors produced by Ramps on the Moon.

As a musician, Paul has toured and recorded extensively. He currently plays guitar in the band Dr. Schwamp.

Joe Douglas, Director

Joe has been Artistic Director of Live Theatre since April 2018. *Clear White Light* marks his first production for the company. Previously he was Associate Artistic Director at Dundee Rep, where he directed *Death of Salesman*, *Spoiling*, *The BFG*, *George's Marvellous Medicine*, *The Resistable Rise of Arturo Ui* and the smash hit revival of John McGrath's *The Cheviot, the Stag and the Black, Black Oil*. He was also Co-Artistic Director of touring company Utter, where he directed *Stand By*, *Bloody Trams* and wrote and performed *Educating Ronnie*. Other work includes *Arabian Nights* (Lyceum), *Letters Home* (Grid Iron), *Dr Stirlingshire's Discovery* (Lung Ha/Grid Iron) and many productions for *A Play, A Pie & A Pint*.

Neil Warmington, Designer

Neil has designed extensively for theatre since graduating from Maidstone college of art with a first-class honours degree in painting.

His credits include *Henry V* (RSC), *Much Ado About Nothing* (Queen's Theatre), *Mary Stuart* and *The Missing* (National Theatre Scotland), *Feverdream* (Citizens Theatre), *Romeo and Juliet*, *Scenes from an Execution*, *Sunshine on Leith* and *Death of a Salesman* (Dundee Rep), *the Vortex* (Kingston), *Gagarin Way*, *Girl in the Machine* and *Passing Places* (Traverse), *Ghosts* and *Loves Labours Lost* (English Touring Theatre), *Jane Eyre* (Young Vic) and *Glass Menagerie* (Lyceum). Neil has also designed operas *Troilus and Cressida* (Royal Opera House) and for Opera North, Connecticut State Opera and has been awarded 4 TMA awards for Best Design.

Max Roberts, Dramaturg

Max is the Emeritus Artistic Director and a founding member of Live Theatre. Over the years Max has worked with some of the country's finest playwrights, many with strong connections to the North East region including C.P. Taylor, Tom Hadaway, Alan Plater, Julia Darling, Pater Straughan, Lee Hall, Michael Chaplin David Almond, Paddy Campbell, Shelagh Stephenson and Patrick Marber. Max's recent productions for the company include *The Red Lion*, which premiered at Live Theatre before transferring to London's West End, and was nominated for an Olivier Award 2018 for Outstanding Achievement in an Affiliate Theatre, *Harriet Martineau Dreams of Dancing* by Shelagh Stephenson, *The Savage* by David Almond adapted from his novel, and *Wet House* by Paddy Campbell which won a host of Newcastle Journal Culture Awards, including Best Production, and transferred to London's Soho Theatre. His latest production for the company, *My Romantic History* by D.C. Jackson – which Max adapted and relocated in Newcastle was hugely popular.

In 2014 Max was awarded an honorary doctorate of letters from Northumbria University as an acknowledgment of his work in theatre and in 2016 he was given a professorship at Sunderland University. In 2011 Max received the Journal Culture Award's Special Contribution Award which was given to honour his achievements in bringing national and international recognition to the work of Live Theatre.

Ali Hunter, Lighting Designer
Ali lights for theatre, dance and opera and her recent credits include *13.60* (Barking Broadway), *The War on Terry* (Landor Space), *The Boatswain's Mate* (Arcola), *The Play About my Dad* (Jermyn Street Theatre), *The Biograph Girl* (Finborough), *Isaac Came Home from the Mountain* (Theatre503), *Gracie* (Finborough), *Tune-D In* (The Place), *Woman Before a Glass* (Jermyn Street Theatre), *The Acid Test* (The Cockpit Theatre), *Doodle* (Waterloo East Theatre), *Cause* (Vault Festival) *Empty Beds and Moments* (Hope Theatre), *Rattlesnake* (Open Clasp), *Tenderly* (New Wimbledon Studio), *Katzenmusik* (Royal Court JTU) and *Foreign Body* (Women of the World and Vault Festival).
Ali is the Young Associate Lighting Designer for the upcoming Matthew Bourne Production.

Dave Flynn, Sound Designer
Dave trained in Media Production at Newcastle College before working in theatre, events and live music as a Sound Engineer and AV Technician.
He started working for Live Theatre in 2001 and became Technical Manager in 2003. His Sound Design credits for Live Theatre include *My Romantic History*, the Olivier-nominated *The Red Lion* (Live Theatre/Trafalgar Studios, London), *The Savage*, *Harriet Martineau Dreams of Dancing*, *Flying into Daylight*, *Wet House* (Live Theatre/Hull Truck/Soho Theatre), *Cooking with Elvis*, *Faith and Cold Reading*, *A Walk on Part* (Live Theatre/Soho Theatre/Arts Theatre London) and *A Northern Odyssey*.

Lucy Jenkins CDG & Sooki McShane CDG, Casting Directors

For Live Theatre casting includes *My Romantic History*, *The Red Lion*, *Harriet Martineau Dreams of Dancing*, *The Savage*, *What Falls Apart*, *A Walk On Part*, *Flying into Daylight*, *Tyne*, and *Wet House*.

West End casting includes *The Play That Goes Wrong*, *Comedy About a Bank Robbery*, *Kite Runner*, *Bomber's Moon* and *War Horse* (all also on Tour).

Other casting credits include *The Last Ship*, *Frankie and Johnny* (Northern Stage), *Jekyll & Hyde* (Tour), *Railway Children* (Tour), *Home Truths* (Cardboard Citizens), *Damned United* (Red Ladder), *Alice in Winterland* (Rose) and *Short History of Tractors in Ukrainian* (Hull Truck).

Film credits include *Transience*, *For Love or Money*, *Widow's Walk* and *Comedian's Guide to Survival*.

ABOUT LIVE THEATRE

Live Theatre has an international reputation as a new writing theatre. As well as producing and presenting new plays, it seeks out and nurtures creative talent.

'One of the most fertile crucibles of new writing'
The Guardian

A high proportion of Live Theatre's work regularly tours to other venues across the UK and internationally, including to Broadway and the Melbourne Festival. *Our Ladies of Perpetual Succour*, written by Lee Hall and co-produced with National Theatre of Scotland, won an Olivier Award for Best New Comedy in 2017 and *The Red Lion* by Patrick Marber, starring Stephen Tompkinson, was nominated for an Olivier Award 2018 for Outstanding Achievement in an Affiliate Theatre.

Live Theatre's work with young people was recognised with an Outstanding Contribution Award at the North East Youth Work Awards and awarded Investors in Children status for its child-led approach. It has the largest free drama education and participation programme in the region.

'Live Theatre is British Theatre's best kept secret.
[It] has supported generation after generation of new writers,
actors and theatre artists.'
Lee Hall, Playwright

Located on Newcastle upon Tyne's Quayside, the theatre is based in a carefully restored complex of five Grade II listed buildings, combining state-of-the-art facilities in a unique historical setting with a flexible and welcoming theatre space, studio, rehearsal room and writers' rooms.

Live Theatre draws on a broad portfolio of income streams and is recognised as a national leader in developing new strategies for increasing income and assets. These include The Schoolhouse, a hub for creative businesses; Live Garden, a beautiful outdoor performance space; Live Tales, a centre for children and young people's creative writing; and Live Works, a commercial office building which has won architectural awards from RIBA and the Civic Trust. Live Theatre receives a percentage of the income from award-winning gastro pub The Broad Chare and from Head of Steam, Quayside.

Live Theatre is funded by Arts Council England as a National Portfolio Organisation, and receives financial support from Newcastle City Council through the Newcastle Culture Investment Fund managed by the Community Foundation, and from other trusts and foundations, corporate partners and Friends.

For more information see **www.live.org.uk**

LIVE THEATRE STAFF

Chief Executive **Jim Beirne**
Emeritus Artistic Director
Max Roberts
Artistic Director **Joe Douglas**
PA to CEO and Finance Assistant
Clare Overton

Customer Services
Customer Service Team Leader
Nichola Ivey
Duty Manager **Grace Blamire**
Duty Manager **Michael Davies**
Duty Manager **Lewis Jobson**
Duty Manager **Ben Young**

Creative Programme
Creative Producer
Graeme Thompson
Creative Programme Administrator
John Dawson
Creative Associate Programming
Anna Ryder

Children and Young People
Children and Young People's
Programme Leader **Helen Green**
Senior Creative Associate Children
and Young People **Paul James**
Creative Associate Children and
Young People **Toni McElhatton**
(maternity leave)
Live Tales Co-ordinator **Saffron Mee**
Creative Associate CYP (Maternity
Cover) **Becky Morris**
Live Tales Volunteer Coordinator
Izzie Hutchinson

Technical & Production
Production Manager
Drummond Orr
Technical & Digital Manager
Dave Flynn
Technician **Craig Spence**

Operations & Finance
Operations Director **Jacqui Kell**
Finance Manager **Antony
Robertson**
Finance Officer **Catherine Moody**

Development
Director Development & Enterprise
Lucy Bird
Development & Events Officer
Caitrin Innis

Marketing & Communications
Marketing & Communications
Manager **Cait Read**
Marketing & Communications
Officer (Digital) **Lisa Campbell**
Marketing & Communications
Officer (CRM & Data) **Kate Stacey**

Friends of Live Theatre

Live Theatre is grateful to our Best Friend donors, whose generosity underpins our core work: producing new writing, providing free arts programmes for children and young people and supporting up-and-coming artists with free training and mentorships.

Anthony Atkinson
Noreen Bates
Jim Beirne
Michael and Pat Brown
Paul Callaghan and Dorothy Braithwaite
George Caulkin
Michael and Susan Chaplin
Sue and Simon Clugston
Helen Coyne
Christine Elton
David and Gitta Faulkner
Chris Foy
Robson Green
Lee Hall
John Josephs
John Jordan
Elaine Orrick
Margaret and John Shipley
Shelagh Stephenson
Sting
Alan Tailford
Graeme and Aly Thompson
Paul and Julie Tomlinson
Lucy Winskell
And others who wish to remain anonymous

Show your support for Live Theatre by joining our fabulous Friends, Good Friends of Best Friends for as little as £5 a month.

**For more information and to join the Friends
call (0191) 269 3499 or see www.live.org.uk/friends**

CLEAR WHITE LIGHT

Paul Sirett

CLEAR WHITE LIGHT

Inspired by the songs of Alan Hull
and
The Fall Of The House Of Usher
by Edgar Allan Poe

OBERON BOOKS
LONDON

WWW.OBERONBOOKS.COM

First published in 2018 by Oberon Books Ltd
521 Caledonian Road, London N7 9RH
Tel: +44 (0) 20 7607 3637 / Fax: +44 (0) 20 7607 3629
e-mail: info@oberonbooks.com
www.oberonbooks.com

Copyright © Paul Sirett, 2018

Lyrics © Alan Hull, Lindisfarne. Reproduced with permission of Hal
Leonard Europe Limited.

Paul Sirett is hereby identified as author of this play in accordance with
section 77 of the Copyright, Designs and Patents Act 1988. The author
has asserted his moral rights.

All rights whatsoever in this play are strictly reserved and application for
performance etc. should be made before commencement of rehearsal to
Independent Talent, 40 Whitfield St, Bloomsbury, London W1T 2RH.
No performance may be given unless a licence has been obtained, and
no alterations may be made in the title or the text of the play without the
author's prior written consent.

You may not copy, store, distribute, transmit, reproduce or otherwise
make available this publication (or any part of it) in any form, or
binding or by any means (print, electronic, digital, optical, mechanical,
photocopying, recording or otherwise), without the prior written
permission of the publisher.

A catalogue record for this book is available from the British Library.

PB ISBN: 9781786826633
E ISBN: 9781786826664

Cover image: Michael Cranston

Printed and bound by 4EDGE Limited, Hockley, Essex, UK.
eBook conversion by Lapiz Digital Services, India.

Visit www.oberonbooks.com to read more about all our books and to buy them. You
will also find features, author interviews and news of any author events, and you can
sign up for e-newsletters so that you're always first to hear about our new releases.

Printed on FSC accredited paper

10 9 8 7 6 5 4 3 2

Characters

ALISON, 20s

ROD, 40s/50s

MADDIE, 40s/50s

plus 4 actor/musicians to play:

JO (Nurse – Female – 20s)

CHARLIE (Patient – Male – 20s)

BARRY (Patient – Male – 50s)

AARON (Patient – Male - 20s) & DOCTOR

A note on the set

At the start of the play ALISON points out a crack in the façade of the hospital; she later sees another crack inside the hospital. During the play these cracks slowly, almost imperceptibly, begin to widen, until by the end of the play…well, you'll see when you get there…

Songs

ACT ONE

ALRIGHT ON THE NIGHT

CITY SONG

SCARECROW SONG

PASSING GHOSTS

LADY ELEANOR

ACT TWO

A WALK IN THE SEA

JANUARY SONG

COURT IN THE ACT

DINGLY DELL

WINTER SONG

CLEAR WHITE LIGHT PT. 2

Act One

SCENE 1

Exterior: St. Nicholas's Hospital, Gosforth, Newcastle. A weak streetlight. Otherwise, darkness. Shadows on shadows. ALISON enters. She is wearing a long, winter coat. ALISON is in her 20s.

ALISON: This is a story about something that happened just over three years ago. I was in the second year of my Mental Health Nursing degree at the time. I had a placement at St. Nick's Hospital in Gosforth. It was my first time on an inpatient night shift and I was very nervous. I stood on the ramp up to the main entrance for ages, not quite daring to go inside –

A door suddenly bursts open, ALISON jumps with fright and the stage is momentarily flooded in a bright, white light as a nurse (JO) hurries past ALISON and exits. The light dims again.

A nurse came out. As I watched her walk away I was reminded of a story one of the nurses at Mental Health Concern in Seaton Burn told us when I did my placement there the year before. Apparently, when she'd been a student nurse there'd been a man on the ward where she worked who'd been hoarding jars of Vaseline. He used to go around the wards picking up half-used jars and tubes of Vaseline and hide them under his bed. Nobody thought much of it. What they didn't know, was that he had an escape plan. One night, he stripped totally bare, covered his whole body in Vaseline, head to toe, and ran stark bollock naked to the main entrance hoping to slip out through the automatic doors...literally. One nurse tried to grab him and... And another... Unfortunately, they turn the automatic doors off at night and he ran straight into

7

them – Bam! Eventually they had to throw a blanket over him. As I stood there outside St. Nick's, I half expected to see a man, smeared in Vaseline come running out with half the staff chasing him…

The hospital doors open. A male doctor steps out. He stands for a moment, looking at his mobile. ALISON turns to him.

Hello…

The doctor blanks ALISON. He exits. She sighs.

(To us.) I took a deep breath and walked up to the main doors. And hesitated. Again. I noticed a crack in the wall running in a zigzag pattern from high above the entrance all the way down to the ground. I stood there staring at it, like it was the most interesting thing I'd ever seen. Anything to delay going inside. Pull yourself together, Ali, I said to myself. I had a twelve-hour shift from 8.30 in the evening to 8.45 in the morning to get through – quite how that adds up to twelve hours is a mystery known only to the NHS. I needed to do some positive thinking. Like they teach you in CBT. Locate your *problem* and identify solutions. Problem: three nights on duty in an all-male adult low secure ward at St. Nicholas's Hospital. Solution: a Friday night out with me mates. There you go! Problem solved…

ALISON goes inside the hospital.

SONG 1

Lights up on MADDIE. MADDIE is in her 50s. She is in a different space; a different time. Perhaps she is with a group of friends? Her story is told in song. MADDIE sings:

ALRIGHT ON THE NIGHT

MADDIE:
I CAN TELL WHAT YOU THINK BY THE LOOK
ON YOUR FACE
THE LOOK ON YOUR FACE IS SO MEAN
CAN YOU TELL ME EXACTLY WHAT
IT IS ABOUT ME THAT'S SO UNCLEAN?

I ONLY EVER WANTED TO BE YOUR FRIEND
AND I NEVER WANTED TO BE YOUR SLAVE
SO TAKE ME AS I APPEAR BEFORE YOU
COME AND LIVE WITH ME IN A CAVE

AND IT'LL BE ALL RIGHT
WE'LL HAVE A DRINK ON A FRIDAY NIGHT
IT'LL BE OH SO GOOD
WE'LL DO EVERYTHING THAT I KNOW WE
SHOULD

I CAN SEE IT ALL NOW FALLING INTO PLACE
YOU CAN LEAVE ALL YOUR TROUBLES BEHIND
YOU CAN TELL AT A GLANCE IF YOU LOOK IN
MY FACE
THAT IT'S REALLY WHIPPIN' UP MY MIND

AND IT'LL BE ALL RIGHT
WE'LL HAVE A DRINK ON A FRIDAY NIGHT
IT'LL BE OH SO GOOD
WE'LL DO EVERYTHING THAT I KNOW WE
SHOULD

SO TAKE ALL YOUR FANCY CLOTHES TO THE
RAGMAN
PUT ON YOUR OLD BLUE JEANS
AND TAKE OFF THAT STUPID LOOK ON YOUR FACE
EVERYTHING I SAY I MEAN

AND IT'LL BE ALL RIGHT
WE'LL HAVE A DRINK ON A FRIDAY NIGHT
IT'LL BE OH SO GOOD
WE'LL DO EVERYTHING THAT I KNOW WE
SHOULD (x2)

Instrumental.

AND IT'LL BE ALL RIGHT
WE'LL HAVE A DRINK ON A FRIDAY NIGHT
IT'LL BE OH, SO GOOD
WE'LL DO EVERYTHING THAT I KNOW WE
SHOULD

Lights down on MADDIE and friends.

SCENE 2

Lights up on interior: St. Nick's. An office. ALISON stands in front of ROD. ROD is in his 50s. ROD is sitting. He greets ALISON enthusiastically.

ROD: Am I pleased to see you! There should be three nurses on my ward tonight, not including you, you don't count – you're a student. That's not an insult, by the way, that's how it works. You're not a human being until you've qualified. Anyway, thing is, Lee's done his ankle and Madeline's had to go to Lennox Ward so it's just you and me. It's bloody ridiculous, I'm a Band 5 Staff Nurse and I'm probably going to be the most senior member of staff in the whole building tonight.

Introducing himself.

Rod.

ALISON: Alison. Ali.

ROD: Do you always look this worried, Ali?

ALISON: Sorry. It's my first time on nights.

ROD: Don't worry about it. It'll only get worse. I'm joking. You'll be all right.

He goes to stand, but quickly sits again.

Christ!

ALISON: Something wrong?

ROD: Benign Paroxysmal Positional Vertigo. In other words, I get a bit dizzy if I stand up too quickly. It's nothing to worry about. And it's a lot cheaper than buying a bottle of gin. Right. We'll head along to the ward in a bit for the handover from the day team. Then we'll do the rounds – just a quick check to make sure everyone's okay. I might allocate you a few patients to keep an eye on tonight. You all right with that?

ALISON: Sure.

ROD: It's an adult male ward, you knew that, right?

ALISON: Yes.

ROD: Quite a big spread of ages.

ALISON: How many are there?

ROD: Sixteen at the last count. After the rounds, I'll update the care plans. Then it'll be time for tea and toast and bed and meds. That's for the patients, not us. Unfortunately. They go to bed when they want, within reason. Not later than ten though. Unless *Match of the Day*'s on. Oh, and I let the old fellers keep their socks on, they like that. Then it's just a case of monitoring – physical checks, safety checks. That kind of thing. Depending on what the day team say or if anyone's unwell. One or two of them can be a bit restless, but we don't need to worry unless they start making a racket and waking the others. If one of them starts it can set the whole lot off. We've got a wide range of illnesses – psychosis, schizophrenia, personality disorders, depression, dementia, bipolar. And we're always full.

ALISON: Always?

ROD: Always. If we want to take a new patient and we've no beds, we have to nominate our 'least unwell' patient for discharge. We have to kick one poor sod out so another one can come in. It's not as bad as some places mind, Manchester and Birmingham are always sending patients here. It's bloody ridiculous. Sorry, you'll have to excuse us. I've a tendency to bang on a bit. I care about the work I do. It's not just a job for me, it's personal.

ALISON: No. I understand. It's important to me too. I want to earn my living doing something that matters.

ROD: Earn a living? Steady on. Right, we better get ourselves down to the ward. I'll work out when we can take our breaks depending on what we're looking at. The handover should only take about half an hour, although it can go on longer. If it's Donna we'll still be there tomorrow morning. But don't panic – I've brought some Chocolate Hobnobs. You can't ask for more than that. Hopefully, we won't get any new admissions.

ALISON: Err…

ROD: Go on.

ALISON: Because there's just the two of us, if, like, if someone becomes difficult or violent, what do we do?

ROD: If anything kicks off, I'll deal with it. It's all about de-escalating the violence. If I need help I can call for someone to come from another ward to support us. You don't need to get involved unless there's absolutely no alternative. Okay?

ALISON: Okay. What if I'm…if you're not here?

ROD: If you get into trouble – You've done your breakaway training, yes? How to get out of holds and that?

ALISON: Yes.

ROD: Right. Well, you'll probably not need it but if you do, just get away and find me as quick as you can.

ALISON: Okay.

ROD: At the end of the day, we do what we have to. If someone is punching the shite out of someone else, we don't have to be delicate about it. Obviously, we don't want to harm anyone, but sometimes we have to do things to get the situation back under control. I've been threatened with everything from a garden hoe to a Bic biro in my time. I had a patient come at me last week with a stapler…

ALISON looks worried.

This conversation isn't helping, is it? Sorry, pet. Listen, truth is, it's once in a blue moon that anything really kicks off. So, don't worry. You'll be all right. It's the verbal stuff you need to watch out for. Some of it can be a bit…near the knuckle. Just remember the patients are unwell and sometimes they don't know what they're saying. It can be a bit brutal, just don't take it to heart. Right?

ALISON nods.

Anything else?

ALISON: Is it basically the same routine every night?

ROD: Yes…and no. You can never plan for what might happen. Some nights can be really quiet. Hopefully we'll get a quiet one tonight. Might even get a bit of reading in.

ROD picks up a well-thumbed book – 'The Fall of the House of Usher and Other Writings' by Edgar Allan Poe – and hands it to ALISON.

Okay, where have I put my phone?

ROD looks for his mobile. ALISON reads the inscription in the book.

ALISON: *(Reads the inscription.)* Who's Maddie?

ROD: Maddie? Oh, she's my sister. She gave me that book when she moved to London.

ALISON: Does she still live there?

ROD: No. She stuck it out for a few years, but –

ROD finds his phone.

Got it! Right! Come on. Better get the handover done with.

ALISON hands the book back to ROD and they exit.

SONG 2

Lights up on MADDIE. If possible, we might see a tableau of the handover from day staff to night staff during this song.

CITY SONG

MADDIE:

CITY STREETS I SEE YOUR LIES
I WILL NOT PLAY YOUR GAME
NO LONGER WILL YOU TALK TO ME
YOU THINK I'M GOING INSANE
BUT I FORGOT MY NUMBER
NOW I'M REMEMBERING MY NAME
I'VE BEEN TOO LONG TRAVELLING ON YOUR
TRAIN

YOU TRIED YOUR BEST TO STRANGLE ME
BUT I COULD TAKE THE PAIN
YOU TRIED TO HYPNOTIZE ME
BUT I SEED RIGHT THROUGH YOUR GAME
AND NOW YOUR TATTY TRICKS TO ME
ARE REALLY RATHER TAME
I'VE BEEN TOO LONG TRAVELLING ON YOUR
TRAIN

CITY LIGHTS DON'T SHINE
THEY GLARE
AND YOUR MUSIC DOESN'T SPEAK
IT SWEARS
AND IN YOUR STREETS
THE GIRLS HAVE FORGOTTEN WHY THEY'RE
THERE

SOME DAY SOON I KNOW I'M GOING
MILES AND MILES AWAY
BACK TO THE GARDEN WHERE THE MAGIC
CHILDREN PLAY

AND TO THE COUNTRY LADY
WHO KNOWS MORE THAN I CAN SAY
WHOSE NIGHTS SHINE BRIGHTER THAN YOUR
DAY

AND YOUR CITY LIGHTS DON'T SHINE
THEY GLARE
AND YOUR MUSIC DOESN'T SPEAK
IT SWEARS
AND IN YOUR STREETS
THE GHOSTS HAVE FORGOTTEN WHY THEY'RE
THERE

Lights down.

SCENE 3

The nurses station on an adult male ward in St. Nicholas's Hospital. ROD is updating patient observations on a PC. ALISON is writing in her practice/placement book. She looks up.

ALISON: *(To us.)* After the handover, we did the rounds. I felt a bit sorry for Rod, he was doing three nurses' jobs and he had a student in tow. But he seemed okay. I was just hoping and praying I'd get through the night. Rod delegated me three patients to keep an eye on…

As ROD and ALISON discuss CHARLIE a light comes up on CHARLIE – he is not (yet) in the scene with them.

ROD: Charlie. Student. Not much older than you, I should think. Here, have a look at his care plan. Charlie has a personality disorder. He gets into unhealthy thinking patterns and functioning. He's been severely self-harming since last summer. He's a smashing lad. Very, very clever. IQ of several billion. He was doing Mathematics at uni.

ALISON: Couldn't he get any support?

ROD: He had an outreach worker, but her job got cut and Charlie was left stranded. Poor kid. He gets into this cycle of thinking he's not good enough and that's when the self-harming kicks in. It's…I don't know. Things just spiraled, and the poor kid ended up getting sectioned. He was on constant observation when he was first in but it's down to two hours now. He's just about the smartest, kindest, young man you could ever hope to meet.

They step into the scene with CHARLIE.

This is Charlie.

ALISON: Hello, Charlie. I'm Alison, pleased to meet you.

CHARLIE: Hello.

ROD: He's the man to come to if you've any problems with your quadratic equations.

CHARLIE: You're daft.

ROD takes a piece of paper out from his pocket and reads from it.

ROD: $3x^2 - 48 = 0$

CHARLIE: Add forty-eight to both sides. Divide both sides by three. Take the square root of both sides. X is equal to positive four or negative four.

ROD shows the piece of paper to ALISON.

ALISON: Wow!

ROD: And he makes a great cup of tea. Isn't that right, Charlie?

CHARLIE: If you say so.

ROD: I say so. We'll see you later.

ALISON: Nice to meet you, Charlie.

ROD and ALISON turn away. They now discuss a second patient – BARRY. As they talk about him, a light comes up on him in a separate space.

ROD: Barry. Now, Barry used to run a garage on Newton Road, got into trouble about five years ago when some kids set fire to the workshop. No insurance. Had a breakdown. He's had a few episodes since. He's attempted suicide a couple of times.

ALISON: All because of the fire?

ROD: Sort of. He's prone to thinking everyone's out to get him – it's a form of psychosis.

ALISON: And he was fine before?

ROD: As far as I know. The business went under, started drinking, wife left him, friends didn't want to know. It must have seemed like everyone had it in for him. He's still obsessed with cars, mind.

They turn to BARRY.

This is Barry. This man knows more about cars than all the presenters of *Top Gear* put together. Do you have a car, Alison?

ALISON: No.

ROD: Barry will be happy to advise.

BARRY: Don't buy a fucking Citroën.

ROD: You have been warned.

ALISON: Thank you, Barry.

ROD and ALISON turn away. BARRY exits. They now discuss a third patient – AARON. As they talk about him, a light comes up on him in a separate space.

ROD: Aaron. Depression. Referred here from Stockton-on-Tees because they didn't have any beds. Recent episodes of mania. He'd been trying to maintain a career as a freelance journalist while keeping his depression a secret. The people he worked for thought he was a driven, ambitious young man. What they didn't see was a bloke struggling to get up in the morning and sometimes just sitting there in the dark with the curtains drawn all weekend.

ALISON: And this brought on episodes of mania?

ROD: It was the start of it. They found him running down the middle of a the A66 to Middlesbrough a couple of weeks ago. He can be a prickly sod, but really I think he's just desperately lonely.

They turn to AARON.

All right, Aaron?

AARON: Ecstatic, Rodney.

ROD: The name is Roderick.

AARON: Freedom of speech.

ROD: Freedom to wind me up.

AARON: Same thing.

ROD: Alison meet Aaron.

ALISON: Hello, Aaron. I hear you're a journalist.

AARON: I'm in here undercover to write an exposé of what goes on behind closed doors in an NHS psychiatric hospital.

ALISON: Better be careful what I say then.

AARON: You had. But please rest assured that anything you do say will be misquoted and then used against you.

ALISON: Thanks for the warning.

We hear a sudden door slam and shout of 'You're a liar! You're a liar! You're a fucking liar!' (Off.)

ROD: Don't worry, it's only Alan. He likes a bit of a shout at his dad every now and then.

They turn away from AARON. AARON exits. CHARLIE stands nearby.

ALISON: *(Back to us.)* After the rounds we made our way back to the nurses' station. I noticed another crack, like the one outside – this one ran down the wall by the window and along the floor.

(To ROD.) Have you seen this crack?

ROD: Aye. I've told them. But there's no money to fix anything because that bastard Health Secretary, Jeremy Hunt, took over a billion pounds from the NHS capital budget last year to pay for day-to-day running costs – money that's supposed to be for new equipment and repairs. Tea?

ALISON: Please.

ROD: Make us a brew will you Charlie?

CHARLIE: Why do I always have to make the tea?

ROD: Cos I love my tea the way you make it.

CHARLIE: You love your tea the way anyone makes it so long as it's not you has to do it.

ROD: I told you he was smart. Go on…

CHARLIE puts the kettle on and gets some cups from the cupboard.

Good lad.

ALISON: *(To us.)* Rod got on with updating the care plans while I wrote up some notes in my practice journal and did some reading about the CPA framework – the Care Programme Approach. Which is huge, by the way.

BARRY re-enters. He crosses to CHARLIE who is standing waiting for the kettle to boil. ROD sees BARRY.

ROD: You all right there, Barry? Charlie's making us a cup of tea. Do you want one? Can you make Barry a cup of tea, Charlie?

CHARLIE gets another cup. The kettle boils. CHARLIE pours the hot water into the first cup – as he does this, BARRY goes to move another cup and hot water splashes on his fingers. BARRY screams! CHARLIE puts the kettle down and backs away. BARRY throws a cup of hot water at CHARLIE, it misses him and smashes against the wall. ALISON and ROD stand. ROD indicates to ALISON that he will handle it. BARRY has now grabbed the kettle and is advancing on CHARLIE.

BARRY: I'll fuckin' scald yer, you fuckin' retard…I'll fuckin' scar yer!

BARRY threatens to pour the boiling water over CHARLIE. CHARLIE cries out and cowers. ALISON is terrified, but ROD is calm, focussed and alert.

ROD: *(Gently.)* Hey-hey-hey-hey-hey! Slow down there, mister…

ROD slowly crosses to BARRY. ALISON watches. ROD reaches for the kettle, but BARRY turns on him. It looks like he might pour the boiling water over ROD.

Think about it! That is boiling hot water! Come on, what happened just now was an accident…

BARRY turns his attention back to CHARLIE who is coiled on the floor gently whimpering.

You know Charlie. You know he wouldn't want to hurt you. It was an accident.

BARRY turns back to ROD. ROD is calm. Beat. ROD takes out some mints.

Polo mint?

BARRY slowly takes a mint. ROD takes the kettle from BARRY.

What do you call a used car salesman?

BARRY: A cardiologist. I told you that.

ROD: Did you? Damn, I thought I just made it up. Ah, well… Can you make Barry's tea, Ali?

ALISON: Sure.

ROD: Milk, two sugars.

ALISON makes BARRY's tea.

Is your hand all right? Can I see?

ROD inspects BARRY's hand.

Looks fine. Let's stick it under the tap though, eh?

ROD puts BARRY's finger under the cold water tap.

Keep your finger there…

ROD gets a burn dressing form from a cupboard.

(Turning to CHARLIE.) You all right, Charlie? Don't worry. Everything's fine.

ROD dries BARRY's hand and applies the dressing.

I don't think there's any harm done, but I'll put a dressing on, just to be on the safe side.

ALISON: Tea's ready.

ROD: How's that for service? I want that cup back. Right?

BARRY takes his tea and goes. ROD turns to CHARLIE.

That wasn't your fault. Right? You still up for making us a cuppa?

CHARLIE nods and goes about making the tea. ALISON cleans up the smashed cup.

Thanks, mate. How do you like your tea, Ali?

ALISON: Milk, no sugar, please.

ROD: Charlie is very safety conscious. Isn't that right, mate. You remember that snow we had after Christmas – well Charlie was the first one out there with a shovel to clear it up. Didn't want anyone getting hurt.

CHARLIE: Only after I'd seen you fall flat on your arse.

ROD: And I thought you were being sympathetic… Oh! I nearly forgot!

ROD takes out some biscuits. Goes to CHARLIE.

Hobnobs! One each.

Conspiring with CHARLIE.

Don't tell Barry.

CHARLIE finishes making the tea. He hands cups to ROD and ALISON.

ALISON: Ta.

ROD: Thanks, mate.

CHARLIE goes back to get his tea. He exits.

See yer later.

ALISON: See you, Charlie.

When CHARLIE has gone…

How did you manage to stay so calm?

ROD: Because you have to. The more normal you can make it seem, the better. De-escalate the conflict. Right, care plans, care plans…

The wind gets up and something crashes to the ground outside. ALISON jumps with fright.

ALISON: What was that?

ROD: Ghost of Byker Bill, probably.

ALISON: …?

ROD: You're not a fan of banshees and apparitions, then?

ALISON: Not exactly.

ROD: Oh, blast, I forgot! I was meant to check Mr Rington's sample. There's a… Can you get us his urine sample, it's in the fridge…

ALISON opens the fridge. She finds a urine sample.

ALISON: This one?

ROD: What's it say on it?

ALISON: Mr Rington.

ROD: That's it. Can you check it to see if he's been taking his meds?

ALISON: I'm not sure I know how…

ROD: Have a sniff. If it smells sort of pepperminty, you'll know he's been taking them.

ALISON: Oh… Really?

ROD: Do they not teach you anything at that university of yours? God, I don't know! Go on. I have to update his care plan.

ALISON unscrews the top of the sample and tentatively sniffs.

Well?

ALISON: It's…er… Yes, it does…smell a bit pepperminty…

ROD: Are you sure?

ALISON: I think so.

ROD: Give it here…

She hands it over. He sniffs it like a connoisseur.

Hmm… Definite, peppery, minty odour…

He takes another sniff. Then, to ALISON's utter astonishment, he takes a sip of the urine and sloshes it around in his mouth. He gargles. He looks for somewhere to spit. There isn't anywhere, so he swallows. ALISON is aghast.

Ahhh! Yes. He's been taking his meds, all right. Here, have a taste…

He holds out the sample for her. She takes it. She hesitates. ROD giggles. She realises she's been had.

ALISON: Oh, you bastard!

ROD takes the sample from her and knocks it back.

ROD: Ah! Ringtons Peppermint Infusion.

ALISON: Did you put that in there just to get me?

ROD: No. We had a bunch of students in a while back and me and Madeline, one of the other nurses, we were going to wind them up by doing a urine tasting session. But we had a new admission and there wasn't time. There's a Mr Tetley and a Mr Typhoo in there and all.

Another bang from outside.

There's a proper storm blowing up out there tonight. Stuffy in here, though. What was is Brian used to say – the air in this place smells like someone just threw up in a bucket of disinfectant. Very lyrical was our Brian.

ALISON: Who's Brian?

ROD: Used to work here. Got sick of the hours and the pay freeze.

ALISON: How long have you been a nurse?

ROD: Five-six years, now. I came to it quite late. Used to work in hospitality. From hospitality to hospitals.

ALISON: What made you decide to be a nurse?

ROD: My sister.

ALISON: She's a nurse?

ROD: No. I used to visit her here.

ALISON: She was in here? A patient?

ROD: Still is. Over ten years now. She was in and out for a bit before that, but...yes, ten years now. I got friendly with one or two of the nurses and, er... Well, to be honest, the hospitality sector wasn't really doing it for me.

ALISON: I'm sorry to hear about your sister.

ROD: Thanks.

ALISON: What is it she's...her diagnosis?

ROD: She's schizophrenic. First diagnosed when she was in her thirties.

ALISON: Do you know why?

ROD: Could be anything. Genetics, drugs...

ALISON: Drugs?

ROD: She was a bit of a hippy. And I think there might have been, perhaps something that went on when she was younger.

ALISON: How do you mean?

ROD: We lost our mam when we were bairns. And we never knew our dad. We were put up for adoption, but no one wanted to take both of us, so we were in care for ages and then when we did get adopted they separated us. We moved heaven and earth to see each other, mind, but, you know...

ALISON: You think something happened to her?

ROB: I don't know. But as an adult she was always doing things to help young lasses, especially if she thought they were vulnerable.

ALISON: Does she talk about any of it?

ROD: Hasn't spoken for years. She's developed a progressive form of catalepsy – stares, doesn't speak, doesn't move. She's in a ward where there are very poorly people. In the beginning she'd have these sudden transformations, from being totally immobile to being in a kind of frenzy. She'd be like that for two or three hours and then, *bang,* she'd be gone again. Catatonia's pretty rare these days, but my sister was always a bit different.

ALISON: It must be hard for you.

ROD: It's not easy, I'll grant you that. The doctors don't know what to do with her. Breaks my heart. She just lies there. Wasting away. Worst of it is, she doesn't even respond to music. Not anymore. She used to love her music. Always singing something… Right! How are your culinary skills?

ALISON: Poor to moderate.

ROD: That's good enough for me. Put some bread in the toaster, put the kettle on and we'll get this lot to bed.

ALISON turns to go. Suddenly, she is face to face with MADDIE who has appeared as if from nowhere. ALISON is taken aback. ALISON turns to ROD, but ROD isn't looking.

ALISON: Rod…

ROD: Yes?

ALISON turns to where MADDIE was standing, but she has gone.

ROD: Yes?

ALISON: There was a woman.

ROD: …?

ALISON: Here. Just now.

ROD: Who?

ALISON: I don't know.

ROD: Probably just wandered in from another ward.

ALISON: …Yes…

ROD: I can have a look, if you / like…

ALISON: No, no it's… I'm fine. She surprised me, that's all.

ROD goes to look out of the window.

ROD: It's like the end of the world out there. Come on, tea and toast and bed and meds.

ROD and ALISON exit.

SONG 3

Lights up on MADDIE. She sings:

SCARECROW SONG

MADDIE:
    THE SONGS YOU SING ARE MEANINGLESS
    THE WORDS YOU SAY ARE WRONG
    YOUR SATURDAY NIGHTS THEY ARE SOBER
    AND YOUR SUNDAYS ARE TOO LONG

    YOUR LUCKY DAYS ARE OVER
    YOUR LUCKY DAYS ARE GONE

    YOU'VE CAST AWAY YOUR COLOURED COAT
    THE ILLUSIONS SEEMED TOO STRONG
    NOW IN THE WINTERY SEASON
    YOU CAN HEAR THE SCARECROW SONG

    YOUR LUCKY DAYS ARE OVER
    YOUR LUCKY DAYS ARE GONE

    THE BELLS HAVE ALL STOPPED THEIR RINGING
    THE MUSIC SOUNDED WRONG
    AND NOW THE ONLY SONG, WORTH SINGING
    IS THE SAD OLD SCARECROW SONG

    YOUR LUCKY DAYS ARE OVER
    YOUR LUCKY DAYS ARE GONE

Lights down on MADDIE.

The hospital.

Lights up on ALISON.

ALISON: *(To us.)* I was checking the patients Rod asked us to keep an eye on. Barry the garage man was sitting up in bed, reading a car magazine…

Lights up on BARRY reading a car magazine.

Everything all right, Barry?

BARRY: No.

ALISON: What's the problem?

BARRY: Jeremy Clarkson.

ALISON: Oh?

BARRY: Listen to this, this is Clarkson on the Ferrari F430 Speciale: 'It was a bit wrong…that smiling front end…it looked like a simpleton…it should have been called the 430 Speciale Needs…' Jeremy Clarkson. What. A. Cunt.

ALISON: Yes. He is a bit, isn't he…

The smile in agreement. Lights down on BARRY. ALISON turns back to the audience.

Next, I looked in on Aaron. He was snoring his head off.

Lights up on AARON snoring. Lights down. ALISON turns back to the audience.

Then, I went into young Charlie's room, but he wasn't in his bed…

Lights up on CHARLIE's darkened room.

Charlie?

CHARLIE is revealed – silhouetted against the wall in the darkness.

You all right, Charlie? Do you mind if I turn the light on?

ALISON turns the light on. CHARLIE stands against the wall, his arms streaked with blood. In his hand, he is holding a piece of sharp plastic he has broken off from his window sill. ALISON does her best to stay clam – but you can see she is struggling to keep a lid on the panic.

Okay. Charlie. Do you want to put that down?

CHARLIE doesn't budge.

No. Right…Please? Perhaps give it to me? Yes?

She steps towards him. CHARLIE steps away.

It's all right, Charlie, I'm not angry…I just want to see what you've got there…

ALISON holds out her hand. CHARLIE remains motionless.

Can I see?

CHARLIE holds out a sharp piece of plastic he has broken off from the windowsill. ALISON takes it.

Thanks. Can I have a look at your arm?

ALISON inspects the cuts.

I'm calling Rod, okay? Yes?

Calls into the corridor.

Rod… Rod…

ALISON gets a clean dressing and applies direct pressure to the deepest of the cuts. At the same time, she slightly raises CHARLIE's arm to reduce the flow of blood to the area. ROD enters.

Charlie's cut himself.

CHARLIE: I'm sorry.

ROD: *(Calmly.)* You all right, Charlie?

ALISON: I don't think it's deep. He had this piece of plastic –

ROD: *(To CHARLIE – about the cuts.)* Can I see?

ROD inspects CHARLIE's arms.

Come on, let's get that arm seen to. Hold it up, there's a good lad…

Lights down on CHARLIE and ROD as they exit.

ALISON: *(To us.)* We took him to the clinical room and I cleaned him up. While I was doing it, I remembered this girl I'd met at a group I used to go to. She used to cut herself. One of the other people in the group asked her why she did it and she told them it was because it made her feel better. She said if she was feeling depressed because of something, the sight of her own blood used to make her feel back in control. It kind of distracted her. She'd done CBT, I think, and had stopped by the time we knew her, but, I think, knowing that helped us to understand Charlie a bit better. When we were done, Rod went to the nurses' station and I took Charlie back to his room…

CHARLIE returns bandaged and cleaned up. He sits calmly. ALISON is now back with CHARLIE in his room.

You okay?

CHARLIE: I'm sorry.

ALISON: You've nothing to be sorry for.

CHARLIE: I'm bad.

ALISON: No, Charlie. You're not bad. Just forget it. Okay?

She closes the window in CHARLIE's room.

There we go. If you want anything, I'm just down the corridor. I'll drop by again in a few minutes. I want to see you in that bed. Okay?

CHARLIE: I'm a bad person –

ALISON: No, Charlie. You're not. You have to be a really good person to think you're a bad person…

Beat.

Does that make sense?

CHARLIE: *(Recovering a little.)* Not really…

ALISON smiles. CHARLIE smiles.

ALISON: Just tell those negative thoughts to get lost and remind yourself how clever you are. Yes?

CHARLIE nods.

I'll be back in a bit.

ALISON leaves. Lights down on CHARLIE. Lights up on the nurses' station. ROD is working. ALISON enters.

ROD: Well done.

ALISON: I don't know about that.

ROD: You didn't panic.

ALISON: It was close.

ROD: No, you did well. Most new nurses would have hit the emergency button and then the whole bloody ward would have gone off.

ALISON: *(Holding out the piece of plastic that CHARLIE used to cut himself with.)* He broke this off the windowsill.

34

ROD takes the piece of plastic from her.

ROD: I better go and have a look.

ALISON: You're all right, it's the outside sill, I locked the
window, he can't get at it.

ROD: You're good at this.

ALISON: Am I?

ROD: If tonight's anything to go by.

As he writes.

I'm going to write in the incident report that you did a
good job. And I'll put a commendation in the feedback for
your tutor.

ALISON: Thanks.

ROD: Poor old Charlie, he's been working so hard to stop self-
harming. He'll be angry with himself in the morning.

ALISON: If only I'd got there five minutes earlier perhaps I
could / have stopped him...

ROD: Hey, don't go blaming yourself for any of this. In fact,
it's probably my fault. I should've taken you off his case
after the kettle thing. I could see he was agitated. I've seen
him like it before. I should have said something. So, don't
blame yourself.

ALISON: Thanks.

ROD goes to stand but gets dizzy again and sits back down.

All right? Do you want some water or –

ROD: Please.

ALISON gets ROD a cup of water and hands it to him.

35

Thanks.

ALISON: Do you want to take a nap?

ROD: Hey, I'm supposed to be keeping an eye on you, remember. No, I'll be all right.

A loud bang from off – perhaps the storm, perhaps a patient. They both jump.

Christ! What was that?

ALISON: Byker Bill's Back.

ROD gets back to working. ALISON looks through paperwork and notices drawings.

Have you seen these?

ROD: Eh?

ALISON: Drawings…

ROD: Ah… Yes… They're mine…

ALISON: You drew these?

ROD: Guilty.

ALISON: They're good.

ROD: Thanks.

ALISON: *(Referring to a specific drawing.)* What's this? There's like a long tunnel, with a really bright light and white walls. Is it underground?

ROD: It might be, said the artist, enigmatically.

ALISON: It's like there's no way out.

ROD: There never is, said the artist, with great pain in his voice.

ALISON: You should take it seriously. They're really good. Honestly.

ROD: Thank you.

ALISON: *(Another picture.)* Is this? It looks like this place, but it's all decaying and falling down…

ROD: Do you like poetry?

ALISON: I suppose. I'm no expert.

ROD: They were inspired by a poem. Well, a short story really, but there's a poem, sort of song, in the middle of it.

Holds up the book of short stories by Edgar Allan Poe.

In here. *The Fall of the House of Usher and Other Writings* by Edgar Allan Poe.

ALISON: I don't know it.

ROD: My sister's favourite book. When she was first in here I used to sit and read it to her. She loved that poem. Here you go…

ROD opens the book.

(Starts reciting the poem from the book.)
In the greenest of our valleys,
By good angels tenanted,
Once a fair and stately palace –
Radiant palace – reared its head.
In the monarch Thought's dominion –

BARRY enters. ROD continues with his poem.

It stood there!

BARRY waits.

Never seraph spread a pinion
Over fabric half so fair.

37

BARRY: Rod…

ROD: Banners yellow, glorious, golden…
　　On its roof did float and flow:

BARRY: Can I have me PRN?

ROD: This – all this – was in olden
　　Time long ago

BARRY: Rod?

ROD gets up and crosses to a medicine cabinet.

ROD: Verily, Barry, I shall get thee thy meds…

ROD unlocks the cabinet and hands some meds to BARRY.

And now you must go back to bed
I shall take you to your room

To ALISON.

Do not despair, I'll be back soon…

ROD exits with BARRY.

(As he exits.)
Come this way, said Rod to Barry
Quickly, sir, do not tarry
– I like that –
Come along, 'tis time to slumber
And dream a dream of a cucumber
– maybe not…

ALISON reads the book. A window suddenly clatters open and a blinding light momentarily flashes across the stage. ALISON shields her eyes from the light. She closes the window. When she turns back into the room, MADDIE is there. ALSION is startled but manages to compose herself.

ALISON: *(To MADDIE.)* You okay? Can I get you anything?

MADDIE doesn't respond. ALISON reaches out and puts a hand on MADDIE's shoulder. MADDIE grabs her wrist. MADDIE is very strong.

Would you...Can you let go. You're very strong...

MADDIE stares deeply into ALISON's eyes.

You're hurting me.

MADDIE lets go of ALISON. ALISON composes herself again.

Which ward are you on?

MADDIE continues to stare at ALISON.

Which –

MADDIE: It's not your fault.

ALISON: What?

MADDIE: The water took him.

ALISON steps away.

The waves.

ALISON is shocked.

You didn't kill him.

ROD re-enters.

ROD: Right! Where were we?

ALISON turns to look at ROD. When she turns back to where MADDIE was, MADDIE has gone. ROD can see that ALISON is unnerved.

Are you all right?

ALISON: She was here again.

ROD: Who?

ALISON: The woman. She said things.

ROD: Like what?

ALISON: Things…

ROD: I told you – don't take any notice. They say all sorts.

ALISON: …

ROD: She's really upset you, hasn't she?

ALISON: I don't know. It was all a bit… There was a really…
bright light at the window and…

ROD: There's nothing out there. Only the garden. Mind, that
was where they built the gallows to hang Byker Bill.

ALISON: Rod!

ROD: Sorry! There were no gallows. You saw a light?

ALISON: It was blinding.

*ROD crosses to the window and opens it. He leans out and lifts up
the remnants of a broken external flood light.*

ROD: External flood light. Wall mounting's broken. Place
is falling to bits. Cheapest tender they could get. All the
fixtures and fittings are stuck together with Blu Tack and
gaffer tape. Don't look so worried…

A NURSE (JO) enters.

NURSE: Rod, you better come.

ROD: What is it?

NURSE: Just…something…

ROD: There's no need to be cryptic.

NURSE: Your sister.

ROD: Maddie?

To ALISON.

Will you be all right on your own?

ALISON: Yes.

ROD: I'll be as quick as I can.

ROD exits with the nurse. Guitar underscoring from 'Passing Ghosts' begins.

SONG 4

MADDIE appears in the space. ALISON continues to read as MADDIE sings:

PASSING GHOSTS

MADDIE:
    YOU CAN SLEEP WITH ME
    WHO'LL SLEEP WITH WE
    WE'LL SLEEP TOGETHER

    YOU DON'T HAVE TO WATCH THE DAWN
    BUT YOU CAN IF YOU WANT

    AND HE CAN SLEEP WITH HER
    WHO'LL SLEEP WITH WE
    WE'LL SLEEP TOGETHER

    YOU DON'T HAVE TO TOUCH THE RAIN
    AND YOU DON'T HAVE TO TALK ABOUT THE
    WEATHER
    COS IT'S ONLY PASSING TIME
    WELL, IT'S ONLY PASSING TIME
    WELL, IT'S ONLY PASSING A LITTLE BIT OF TIME

Guitar continues under the scene. ROD re-enters. ALISON is shaken from her somnambulant trance.

ALISON: Everything okay?

ROD: She's dead. My sister.

ALISON: Oh. Rod, I'm so sorry.

ROD: Yes. Thanks.

ALISON: Is there anything I can do?

ROD: No. Yes. You can help us to move the body.

ALISON: Me?

ROD: I have to take her down to the mortuary.

ALISON: Is that… What about the ward here?

ROD: Jo's gone to have a word. She'll get someone to cover. She'll be back in a minute.

ALISON: Are you sure about taking her?

ROD: I don't want no one else touching her. It's important to me. I didn't get to say goodbye. I should have gone. I should have gone tonight.

ALISON: It's not your fault, Rod?

ROD: Isn't it?

ALISON: There was nothing you could have done.

ROD: I could have been there. I could have done… something… I promised I'd be there for her…

The NURSE re-enters.

NURSE: Rod…

ROD: Right.

NURSE: Tony'll help you take her down.

42

ROD: I want Ali to do it.

NURSE: I'm not sure that's appropriate –

ROD: It is, if I say it is. Just keep an eye on things here for us.

NURSE: Okay.

ROD exits. ALISON follows. MADDIE appears in the space again. She concludes singing 'Passing Ghosts'.

MADDIE:
AND WHEN MY TIME HAS COME
MY CALL HAS TIME
TO COME TOGETHER

AND IF MY GRAVE IS REALLY STILL
I WON'T NEED TO TALK ABOUT THE WEATHER
COS IT'S ONLY PASSING TIME
WELL, IT'S ONLY PASSING TIME
WELL, IT'S ONLY PASSING A LITTLE BIT OF TIME

Lights down on MADDIE.

SCENE 5

The hospital mortuary. It is poorly lit. We hear a beep and the sound of a door unlocking. Bright, white light floods in through a heavy door as ALISON and ROD heave it open and enter, pushing a body in a body bag on a trolley. There is a three-tiered fridge for bodies. ROD checks the lights – they don't seem to be working. He checks the fridge; ALISON turns to us. SFX of entering the mortuary, door, etc, underscores her speech.

ALISON: *(To us.)* The mortuary is underground. It's reached along a white corridor like the one in Rod's drawing. It's lit by bright fluorescent tubes. It was quite dark inside. I think the sensor was broken or something. But we had the light from the corridor, so we could see what we were doing…

ROD slowly unzips the body bag. He stares at MADDIE for a while.

ROD: *(Talking to the body.)* What happened, eh, Maddie?

ROD leans in and fully embraces the corpse.

You took on too much pain. You cared too much. You were too good, Maddie. Too good.

ROD pulls away from MADDIE.

(To ALISON.) She still has some colour in her cheeks, look. It usually all drains out when people pass on.

ALISON looks at the corpse. She looks at ROD, then back at the corpse. Then back at ROD.

ALISON: It's her.

ROD: What?

ALISON: Her. The woman I saw on the ward.

ROD: Can't have been.

ALISON: It is. I swear it.

ROD: She's not got out of bed unaided for twelve months.

ALISON: It was her, Rod. I swear it was.

ROD: *(Insistent.)* It can't have been!

ALISON: Okay.

ROD: Don't say things like that.

ALISON: Okay, sorry.

ROD: She couldn't move.

ALISON: It's just, she… I'm sorry, Rod. The light in here's not great.

ROD: Fine. I didn't mean to have a go.

ALISON: I understand.

ROD: I thought I was prepared. For this.

ALISON: How did she die?

ROD: Heart stopped. Simple as.

ALISON: Was she older or younger than you?

ROD: Older. By fifteen minutes. Never let me forget it.

ALISON: …?

ROD: We're twins.

ALISON: You never said you were twins.

ROD: Yeah… Didn't I? I suppose it's a blessed relief in some ways, this. She hated all the suffering in the world. Used to take it personally. My big sister with the big heart. Too big. She looked after me when I was a speccy kid with no mates. Made sure I was safe. That's why I'm here. Doing this. It was my turn to look after her. I wanted to be there for her. And I wasn't.

ALISON: You weren't to know.

ROD: I've let her down. I'm sorry, Maddie. Please, forgive me.

To ALISON.

She used to say we were all on the brink of going under
in a sea of madness. She could read people like you and
me read a book. Especially young people. She could
read their pain. She could sense if people were carrying
hurt. She'd somehow know what caused their pain. And
she'd take that pain away and carry it herself. It was what
caused her to have the breakdowns. I know it was. It was
probably what killed her…

Pause.

ALISON: Rod?

ROD: Yes?

ALISON: What do mean, she could read people?

ROD: She could tell. If you were suffering. I thought it was
all nonsense at first, some hippy, mystical, dope-smoking
bollocks. But I saw it. I remember this lass at one of her gigs
in Heaton Park. She knew this girl was in pain and she held
her, and I heard her say, 'It's not your fault, pet, I know it's
not. You can give me your pain… I'll carry it.' And the lass
just backed away…she seemed lighter…she looked like she
was…relieved… It became a part of Maddie's existence.
She'd carry the pain of others. That's why she ended up
in here. She'd carried my pain since I was a bairn…cos I
missed me Mam… She's been carrying me and people like
that young lass for years.

ALISON shivers.

Cold?

ALISON: Yes.

46

ROD: *(Looks back at the body.)* Would you look at her? She's smiling. Can you believe it? I haven't seen that smile in years.

He leans in and kisses MADDIE.

Must be the relief, eh Maddie? Is it good on the other side? Are you up there singing songs?

He's cracking up.

Maddie…

He manages to pull himself together. To ALISON.

Come on, let's get this over with.

To MADDIE.

Bye, Maddie… Bye, sweetheart…

ROD kisses MADDIE, pauses for a moment, then zips the body bag back up. The opening guitar and bass from 'Lady Eleanor' plays quietly while they lift the trolley that the body is on and slide it into one of the shelves. ROD closes the door.

ALISON: Rod, don't you think you should go home?

ROD: And do what? Sit in me room staring at the wall thinking about her all night? No, I want to stay. Thanks for helping.

ALISON: That's all right. Are there any family you want me to call?

The mandolin joins the guitar and bass.

ROD: No.

ALISON: In the morning? I can do it then.

ROD: There isn't anyone. Come on…

They turn to go. Was that a scratching sound? They both stop. They exchange a look. They listen. Silence. ROD shakes his head. They exit, pulling the heavy door shut behind them. A beep and click as the door locks. The stage is bathed in a dim light.

Is that more scratching we can hear? And what was that thudding noise? Where did it come from? Surely not from inside where MADDIE was interred?

Music now gently building. Mist starts to seep into the mortuary. Music gets louder leading to…

SONG 5

Lights up on MADDIE. She sings:

LADY ELEANOR

MADDIE:
BANSHEE PLAYING MAGICIAN SITTING LOTUS
ON THE FLOOR
BELLY DANCING BEAUTY WITH A POWER
DRIVEN SAW
HAD MY SHARE OF NIGHTMARES, DIDN'T
THINK THERE COULD BE MUCH MORE
THEN IN WALKED RODRICK USHER WITH THE
LADY ELEANOR

SHE TIED MY EYES WITH RIBBON OF A SILKEN
GHOSTLY THREAD
I GAZED WITH TROUBLE VISION ON AN OLD
FOUR POSTER BED
WHERE ELEANOR HAD RISEN TO KISS THE
NECK BELOW MY HEAD
AND BID ME COME ALONG WITH HER TO THE
LAND OF THE DANCING DEAD

BUT IT'S ALL RIGHT, LADY ELEANOR
ALL RIGHT, LADY ELEANOR
I'M ALL RIGHT WHERE I AM

SHE GAZED WITH LOVING BEAUTY LIKE A
MOTHER TO A SON
LIKE LIVING, DYING, SEEING, BEING ALL
ROLLED INTO ONE
THEN ALL AT ONCE I HEARD SOME MUSIC
PLAYING IN MY BONES
THE SAME OLD SONG I'D HEARD FOR YEARS,
REMINDING ME OF HOME

BUT IT'S ALL RIGHT, LADY ELEANOR
ALL RIGHT, LADY ELEANOR
I'M ALL RIGHT WHERE I AM

THEN CREEPING ON TOWARDS ME, LICKING
LIPS WITH TONGUES OF FIRE
A HOST OF GOLDEN DEMONS SCREAMING
LUST AND BASE DESIRE
AND WHEN IT SEEMED FOR CERTAIN THAT THE
SCREAMS COULD GET NO HIGHER
I HEARD A VOICE ABOVE THE REST
SCREAMING 'YOU'RE A LIAR'

BUT IT'S ALL RIGHT, LADY ELEANOR
ALL RIGHT, LADY ELEANOR
I'M ALL RIGHT HERE IN YOUR ARMS

Song finishes.

End of Act One.

Act Two

Lights up on MADDIE/ROD/ALISON.

A WALK IN THE SEA

MADDIE/ROD/ALISON:
I THINK I'LL GO WALK IN THE RAIN
NOTHING MUCH BETTER TO DO
NO ONE ELSE FEELS THE SAME, NOT EVEN YOU

I LIKE TO BE ON ME OWN
WORK THINGS OUT IN MY OWN MIND
ALL THE PEOPLE I'VE KNOWN, LEAVE THEM
BEHIND

AND IF I MEET MY TWIN SOUL
I KNOW JUST WHERE IT WILL BE
WORDS NOT SPOKEN BUT TOLD INSIDE OF ME

SO ALL MY LIFE I PERCEIVE
I'LL BE TRAPPED IN MY OWN SKIN
BUT THERE'S NO CAUSE TO GRIEVE IF NO ONE
COMES IN

I THINK I'LL GO WALK IN THE SEA
NOTHING MUCH BETTER TO DO
NO, NOTHING FOR ME, NOT EVEN YOU

Lights down.

SCENE 1

Lights up on ALISON and ROD at the nurses' station.

ALISON: Rod, can I ask you something?

ROD: Fire away.

ALISON: About your sister?

ROD: What?

ALISON: I just…

ROD: What?

ALISON: You said she hadn't been out of bed for a while?

ROD: Not without help.

ALISON: I know you said it couldn't have been her / but I really…

ROD: Not this again, Ali-

ALISON: She looked just like her! / I swear!

ROD: No!

ALISON: But it must've / been…

ROD: No!

ALISON: Please, Rod –

ROD: It wasn't her!

ALISON: You don't know that! / You don't…

ROD: Of course I know!

ALISON: She said things to me! / Things she couldn't possibly know! Like that girl you told us about. She said it wasn't

my fault! She knew! She knew! How could she know?
How could she know those things?

ROD: I'm not listening to this. I've work to do. Yes. Yes. Yes.
Yes. Yes. That's enough. Enough, Ali. I said enough!
Enough! Enough! ENOUGH!

ALISON: Please, I need to tell you this.

ROD: MY SISTER HAS JUST DIED!

Pause. ALISON hesitates, then...

ALISON: When I was a kid we used to go to Cornwall.
Camping. Drove there. Mum and Dad would stick us in
in the back of the car at midnight or thereabouts piled
up with pillows and duvets and drive through the night.
Every year. I was... Me brother... The campsite was on
this hill overlooking the bay. Just a short walk down to
the beach. I was out rockpooling with me little brother,
Steven. He was five. Mum and Dad were on the beach,
sunbathing or reading or... I don't know. We wandered
quite a way off. The tide was coming in and I didn't really
notice – we were too busy looking for these little crabs and
what have you. Then I realized we were cut off from the
beach. And I started to panic. The sea was getting rough
and the rocks were... Steven started to cry and I... Well
I knew we couldn't just stand there and wait for the tide
to come in, so I decided we had to climb up a bit to see if
we could get round higher up. The waves were crashing
in by now and the rocks were getting slippery, but we got
a little way up. Then, this almighty wave came smashing
against the cliff. I hung on for all I was worth. But...
when I looked, Steven was gone. I screamed his name.
Screamed until my throat was raw. And I... Then I heard
this voice. Someone...telling us to hold on and... I don't
know how long I was there, but after a while someone
climbed down to get us. And I was just... 'Steven! Steven!'

But he was gone… He couldn't swim and… My parents were inconsolable. They said they didn't blame me. But all my life I've…

ROD: You didn't kill him.

ALISON: That's what she said! Rod. That's exactly what she said!

ROD: How old were you when all this happened?

ALISON: Nine. I had to make a statement. Dad was with me. I can still remember it like it was yesterday. Sat on this hard, wooden chair and this giant of a man with a big, black beard with spit in it asking me questions and writing down whatever I said. His breath smelled sickly, like Dad's when he'd been boozing. I remember him giving me this big sheet of paper with his writing all over it and asking us to sign it. I'd been practicing my autograph for months. That was the first time I ever got to use it.

ROD: I'm sorry, Ali. I didn't mean to… It must have been hard for you…growing up with that…

ALISON: Thank you.

ROD: Look, you're right about Maddie. It does sound like something she might have said… But it couldn't have been her. Really. She hasn't moved a muscle since… I don't see how…

He's getting upset.

I just don't see… I can't talk about this now, Ali. Look, I'm sorry. I've work to do.

Lights down.

SONG 7

Lights up on MADDIE. She sings:

JANUARY SONG

MADDIE:
 I'M FEELING RATHER SORRY
 FOR A MAN I KNOW
 THE WORLD HE HOLDS IN TREMBLING HANDS
 IS ASKING WHERE TO GO

 AND AS HE STARES OUT AT ME
 FROM THE MIRRORED WALL
 I SEE THAT HE IS TRYING TO CRY
 BUT THE TEARS THEY WILL NOT FALL

 HIS LIFE IS PASSING BY BEHIND HIS TIRED EYES
 LIKE THE COLOURS IN THE JANUARY SKY

 USELESS IT IS TO QUESTION
 THINGS CONCERNING THE PAST
 SEEMS SO VERY OBVIOUS
 THAT NOTHING AT ALL CAN LAST

 AND JUST AS SURE AS TOMORROW
 WILL SOON BE YESTERDAY
 THE LOVE YOU THOUGHT TO OCCUPY
 WILL SURELY DRIFT AWAY

 I NEED YOU TO HELP ME CARRY ON
 YOU NEED ME NEED YOU NEED HIM NEED
 EVERYONE

 AND LOVE IS SUCH A SMALL WORD
 FOR SOMETHING THAT IS SO VAST
 BUT IN IT LIES THE FUTURE
 THE PRESENT AND THE PAST

AND SPEAKING NOW OF CHANGES
I SOMETIMES FEEL THE FEAR
THAT THE REASON FOR THE MEANING
WILL EVEN DISAPPEAR

I NEED YOU TO HELP ME CARRY ON
YOU NEED ME NEED YOU NEED HIM NEED
EVERYONE... *(Repeat.)*

Lights down on MADDIE.

Lights up on ROD and ALISON at the nurses' station.

ROD: Greenham Common? The Women's Peace Camp? No? Back in the 80s.

ALISON: I wasn't born.

ROD: No. Well, anyway it was a big protest about American nuclear weapons being sited on the RAF base there. That's when it all started for her. She got arrested and roughed up by the police – called her a witch, a dyke, a madwoman, all sorts. Then there was the Miner's Strike. Greenpeace. You name it she joined it. Anti-fox hunting. Anti-apartheid. Anti-poll tax. I used to call her Anti Maddie sometimes – Here comes Anti Maddie... She got arrested three or four times.

ALISON: What for?

ROD: First time was Greenham, then an anti-apartheid march in London.

ALISON: What happened?

ROD: Got a fine, I think. Then there was the Hunt Saboteurs. She had this boyfriend at the time, Dennis, a Che Guevara lookalike who did a bit of dope dealing on the side. Well, they'd gone to this hunt somewhere and they'd brought along all these spray bottles, all different shapes and sizes filled with this solution they'd concocted to dull the scent of the foxes. Anyway, they're in the middle of this wood and Maddie's just finished laying out all these sprays when she looks up and sees Dennis legging it back to the car. He'd seen the police coming and done a runner. And there was our Maddie, sitting in front of two dozen assorted perfume bottles like a very confused Avon lady. She was caught red-handed. And hunting was legal back then, remember. They hated the sabs. The police wanted names, but she wouldn't talk. She tried to leg it, but they grabbed her and shoved her in the back of a police van. So, there she is, up in court and the judge just happens to be a former hunt master…

ALISON: Oh no…

ROD: Exactly. And he's going on about all these toxic chemicals she was going to spray in the horses' eyes – which she would never do, it was just a bit of lemon and eucalyptus. And then this cop is called to give evidence and he's on about how she resisted arrest and assaulted two officers. Maddie! The least violent person I have ever known. They had it in for her. She got two months.

ALISON: No!

ROD: I kid you not. Poor Maddie, it was hard in there for her. And then, then, a week after she gets out, Dopey Dennis buggers off down south with one of her best friends. People took advantage of her. I tried to tell her. But she wouldn't listen.

ALISON: Did she… Neither of you has kids?

ROD: No. She had plenty of boyfriends, but she never settled.

NURSE: *(Voice off.)* Mr Hutchinson!

The NURSE (JO) enters – she stands in the doorway.

Rod…

ROD: What is it?

The NURSE points along the corridor (behind her). ROD crosses to her.

NURSE: One of your patients would appear to be having an extremely loose bowel movement in the corridor.

ROD: *(Looking along the corridor.)* Oh, Hutch, man…

ALISON: Shall I?

NURSE: You'll need the mop.

ROD: I'll get it.

NURSE: *(To ALISON.)* Did you know that diarrhoea is hereditary?

ALISON: Diarrhoea?

NURSE: Yes, apparently it –

NURSE/ROD: – runs in your genes –

ROD: – Yes, very funny.

To ALISON.

You mop. I'll clean him up.

ROD, ALISON and the NURSE exit.

SONG 8

Lights up on MADDIE. She sings:

COURT IN THE ACT

MADDIE:
GOT THE SUMMONS SERVED ON A SUNDAY,
SEE WHAT I DONE
COULDN'T SEE MUCH SENSE IN THE CHARGES,
BUT THEY SURE SOUNDED LIKE FUN
SO I WENT DOWNTOWN TO A BOW STREET, TO
SEE THE COMPANY MAN
'HEY BOY YOU'RE IN A HEAP OF TROUBLE, BUT
I'LL DO EVERYTHING THAT I CAN'

BUT THE JUDGE IS A GRUDGE MAN, AND
THAT'S A FACT (MAN THAT'S A FACT)
AND THE JUDGE IS A GRUDGE MAN, AND
THAT'S A FACT
YOU SHOULDN'T LET YOURSELF NEVER GET
CAUGHT IN THE ACT

SORRY FOR THE DAMAGE I'VE DONE, TRY TO
PAY IT BACK
THE ONLY CRIME I EVER COMMITTED WAS
BEING CAUGHT IN THE ACT
SO THE NEXT TIME THAT YOU FEEL GOOD
DON'T FORGET THE FACT
THERE'S A MAN IN BLUE AND HE WANTS YOU
TO BE, BE CAUGHT IN THE ACT

AND THE JUDGE IS A GRUDGE MAN, AND
THAT'S A FACT (MAN THAT'S A FACT)
AND THE JUDGE IS A GRUDGE MAN, AND
THAT'S A FACT
HOPE THAT YOU NEVER GET CAUGHT IN THE
ACT

AND THE JUDGE IS A GRUDGE MAN, AND
THAT'S A FACT (MAN THAT'S A FACT)
AND THE JUDGE IS A GRUDGE MAN, AND
THAT'S A FACT
HOPE THAT YOU NEVER GET CAUGHT IN THE
ACT

Percussion underscores as:

ALISON re-enters with the mop and bucket. She is putting it away when AARON and CHARLIE enter. They don't see her. CHARLIE goes to the cupboard where ROD has hidden his Hobnobs. He takes them out.

AARON: Hobnobs! You're a star, Charlie. I'm starving!

CHARLIE: Don't tell Rod.

AARON: Your secret's safe with me. Where is he? Rod?

CHARLIE: He's gone off somewhere with that lass, the new nurse.

BARRY enters.

AARON: Aye-aye Barry there, lad.

BARRY: What you got?

AARON: If you ask nicely, Charlie might give you a Hobnob.

CHARLIE offers the packet to BARRY. BARRY takes one – there is a look between them.

BARRY: Thanks, Charlie. Sorry about before, like…

AARON: Don't tell Rod.

They munch.

BARRY: Hey, that student lass is canny, isn't she?

CHARLIE: Yes, she is.

AARON: We should keep an eye on her. Make sure she's okay.

BARRY: She'll be all right with Rod.

AARON: You're joking. Rod's mad as a hatter.

CHARLIE: At least he's in the right place.

AARON: I wonder where they've gone?

CHARLIE: Perhaps we should do the rounds. Make sure everyone's okay?

AARON: Hand out some medicinal Hobnobs.

BARRY: Great idea.

AARON: Come on.

They exit. ALISON watches them go. Song concludes.

MADDIE:
AND THE JUDGE IS A GRUDGE MAN, AND
THAT'S A FACT (MAN THAT'S A FACT)
AND THE JUDGE IS A GRUDGE MAN, AND
THAT'S A FACT
HOPE THAT YOU NEVER GET CAUGHT IN THE ACT

Lights down on MADDIE.

SCENE 3

Nurses' station. Lights up on ALISON and ROD. ROD is pacing up and down.

ALISON: I think I can manage if you want to go and have a lie down for / a bit…

ROD: / I'm fine.

ROD continues to pace. Then stops, suddenly, and stares ahead – it is as if he is straining to hear something in the distance above the sound of the wind. Was that someone screaming? A woman? A child? ALISON is watching him.

ALISON: Rod?

ROD: Shh!

ROD continues to listen. He exits, suddenly.

ALISON: Rod!

ROD exits. The wind gets up outside.

Underscoring: DINGLY DELL.

ALISON watches ROD through the window. Lights flicker. Lighting state shifts. She places her hand on the wall. The wall seems to expand and contract a little – like lungs. ALISON is not sure if she has felt it or not. We hear screams from outside. ALISON staggers back. ALISON breathes heavily. She feels cold. She starts to shake. She paces. She listens. Was that another scream? She starts exercising – doing whatever she can to distract herself. She stops. She listens. Silence. A sudden loud knocking at a door. A door that hasn't been used during the night so far. ALISON is startled. She crosses to the door. She stands. Silence. Another knock.

Who is it?

Another knock. ALISON hesitates. Another, more insistent knock. ALISON unlocks and opens the door. A beam of light hits her in the face. She staggers back. ROD enters holding a torch which he waves like an axe.

ROD: Here's Johnny!!!

Lighting state snaps back to normal. ALISON is hyperventilating – the early stages of a panic attack.

Hey-hey-hey! It's all right! It's just me. Calm down. Yes? Come on… Breathe… That's it…

ALISON calms herself.

It's all right…

ALISON: You scared me!

ROD: Sorry. I'm sorry.

ALISON: What were you doing? Where have you been?

ROD: I had to get out.

ALISON: In that?

ROD: I thought I heard Maddie…

ALISON: …?

ROD: I'm sorry if I gave you a fright.

ALISON is close enough to smell alcohol on ROD's breath.

ALISON: Have you been drinking?

ROD: Look… Ah, forget it –

ALISON: I don't understand, Rod. What are you saying?

ROD: Me and Maddie… Sometimes, when there was a storm Maddie would grab me and… 'Let's go out, Rod!' And

out we'd go into the back garden or wherever, and…start
screaming.

ALISON: You'd…?

ROD: She'd done all this primal scream stuff where everyone,
you know, stands around and…

Screams playfully.

Arghhh!

ALISON: Was that you, just now? Out there.

ROD: You should try it –

ALISON: I don't think so.

ROD: It's bloody cathartic. Come on…

ROD pulls ALISON towards the door.

ALISON: No, Rod –

ROD: Come on!

ROD wrenches open the door. The storm blasts in.

(Screams – loudly, with passion.) Aaaaaaahhhhhhhhh!!!

*Leaves and debris are blown inside. ROD stands in the doorway,
welcoming the blast of nature. ALISON, on the other hand, is swept
away by the wind and pinned against the wall, terrified.*

*The reality shifts as a luminous mist/vapor blows in on the wind
and begins to seep in through cracks in the walls and the floor, from
cabinets, doorways, computers. Equipment and furniture begin to
glow luminously.*

SONG 9

Lights up on MADDIE. She sings:

DINGLY DELL

MADDIE:
WHERE DID YOU SEE ME LAST?
WAS IT DOWN IN DINGLY DELL?
AND COULD YOU REALLY TELL IF IT WERE I
OR JUST A PASSING BUTTERFLY?

WHERE WILL YOU SEE ME NEXT?
WILL YOU WEAR A RIBBON IN YOUR HAIR?
LOOK AT ME BUT DO NOT STARE
OR I MAY BREAK, EVAPORATE INTO THE AIR

OOH, OOH, OOH – THERE'S MAGIC IN THE AIR
OOH, OOH, OOH – IT'S EVERYWHERE
AND I NEED YOU, TO SHARE IT WITH ME
BUT YOU'RE NOT THERE AND NEVER WILL YOU
BE

OOH, OOH, OOH – THERE'S MAGIC IN THE AIR
OOH, OOH, OOH – IT'S EVERYWHERE
AND I NEED YOU, TO SHARE IT WITH ME
BUT YOU'RE NOT THERE AND NEVER WILL YOU
BE

Lights down on MADDIE.

SCENE 4

Nurses' station.

ROD slams the door shut. (Perhaps the song finishes as he shuts the door?) The luminosity disperses.

ALISON sits. She composes herself.

ROD crosses to the window and stands there for a moment, looking out.

ROD: She lived rough on the streets for a while.

ALISON: Maddie?

ROD: Yes. One Christmas. I couldn't find her anywhere. Some gypsies took her in and looked after her. Gave her Christmas dinner. That was just before she came in here the last time. Can you imagine being out there in that. Nowhere to go.

ALISON: No. Must be hard.

ROD starts to cry. ALISON isn't quite sure what to do.

Rod? I'll go and get one of the other nurses –

ROD: No!

ALISON: I won't be a minute –

ROD: Don't leave me! Please!

ALISON: Okay. Can I get you anything?

ROD: Will you read to me? Like Maddie did?

ALISON: I thought it was you that read to her?

ROD: Not when we were kids. She always read to me then. Before they separated us. Will you?

ALISON: I can try. If that's what you want.

ROD: Yes.

ROD opens the Poe book for ALISON at the page he wants.

From here. The story within the story. The narrator reads it to Usher. The hero of the story is a knight called Ethelred. He's trying to get shelter from this terrible storm where this hermit lives, but the hermit won't let him in, so he tries to force the door open… Okay?

ALISON: Okay. I'll give it go…

ROD: Take your time. Don't rush it.

ALISON: Right…

Reads.

'And Ethelred, who was by nature of a doughty heart…' Doughty?

ROD motions for her to continue.

'…and who was now mighty withal, on account of the powerfulness of the wine which he had drunken, waited no longer to hold parley with the hermit, who, in sooth…'

Wow, this is real olde English…

ROD ignores her remark.

'…who, in sooth, was of an obstinate and maliceful turn, but, feeling the rain upon his shoulders, and fearing the rising of the tempest, uplifted his mace outright…'

ALISON hesitates. ROD is impatient for her to carry on. (NB. Perhaps underscoring for 'Winter Song' starts here?)

Sorry…

'…and, with blows, made quickly room in the plankings of the door for his gauntleted hand, and pulling therewith sturdily, he so cracked, and ripped, and tore all asunder. And in the darkness of the night, the freezing, icy wind did blow, and the noise of the dry and hollow-sounding wood reverberated throughout the forest. And now the good Ethelred, entering within the door, saw the hermit and the beggar, the gypsy and the tramp, outcasts all…'

In the distance we hear a sound of cracking and ripping reverberating like in the story. Did she imagine it? Was it just the storm? She looks at ROD, he is staring at the window. The storm continues to blow. (Or perhaps the door flies open and ALISON closes it? Or a window flies open and she closes it?)

SONG 10

Lights up on MADDIE. She sings:

WINTER SONG

MADDIE:
WHEN WINTER'S SHADOWY FINGERS
FIRST PURSUE YOU DOWN THE STREET
AND YOUR BOOTS NO LONGER LIE
ABOUT THE COLD AROUND YOUR FEET
DO YOU SPARE A THOUGHT FOR SUMMER
WHOSE PASSAGE IS COMPLETE?
WHOSE MEMORIES LIE IN RUINS
AND WHOSE RUINS LIE IN HEAT?
WHEN WINTER...
COMES HOWLING IN

WHEN THE WIND IS SINGING STRANGELY
BLOWING MUSIC THROUGH YOUR HEAD
AND YOUR RAIN SPLATTERED WINDOWS
MAKE YOU DECIDE TO STAY IN BED
DO YOU SPARE A THOUGHT FOR THE
HOMELESS TRAMP WHO WISHES HE WAS DEAD?
OR DO YOU PULL THE BEDCLOTHES HIGHER
DREAM OF SUMMERTIME INSTEAD?
WHEN WINTER...
COMES HOWLING IN

THE CREEPING COLD HAS FINGERS
THAT CARESS WITHOUT PERMISSION
AND MYSTIC CRYSTAL SNOWDROPS
ONLY AGGRAVATE THE CONDITION
DO YOU SPARE ONE THOUGHT FOR THE GYPSY
WITH NO SECURE POSITION?
WHO'S TURNED AND SPURNED BY VILLAGE
AND TOWN

70

AT THE MAGISTRATE'S DECISION?
WHEN WINTER...
COMES HOWLING IN

WHEN THE TURKEY'S IN THE OVEN
AND THE CHRISTMAS PRESENTS ARE BOUGHT
AND SANTA'S IN HIS MODULE
HE'S AN AMERICAN ASTRONAUT
DO YOU SPARE ONE THOUGHT FOR JESUS,
WHO HAD NOTHING BUT HIS THOUGHTS?
WHO GOT BUSTED JUST FOR TALKING
AND BEFRIENDING THE WRONG SORTS?
WHEN WINTER...
COMES HOWLING IN

WHEN WINTER...
COMES...
HOWLING...
IN

Lights down on MADDIE.

SCENE 5

Nurses' station. ALISON continues with the story. (NB. Perhaps continue 'Winter Song' underscore through next speech?)

ALISON: 'But then, of a sudden, all were gone and before him stood a dragon of a scaly and prodigious demeanour, and of a fiery tongue, in guard before a palace of gold, with a floor of silver and upon the wall there hung a shield of shining brass with this legend enwritten –

Who entereth herein, a conqueror hath bin;

Who slayeth the dragon, the shield he shall win.

And Ethelred uplifted his mace, and struck upon the head of the dragon, which fell before him, and gave up his pesty breath,' – 'pesty breath' – I love that! – '...gave up his pesty breath, with a shriek so horrid and harsh, and withal so piercing, that Ethelred had fain to close his ears with his hands against the dreadful noise –'

We hear a harsh, protracted screaming like that narrated in the story – there is no doubt that it is real. ALISON is unnerved, but this is a hospital and cries and shouts are not unusual...

ROD has not reacted to the noise, but he now picks up his chair and goes to sit facing the main door into the ward. He is trembling and murmuring something indecipherable to himself.

Rod?

ROD drops his head onto his chest. ALISON crosses to him.

Rod?

Has he fallen asleep? No. His eyes are wide open. ROD lifts his head and starts to rock gently back and forth in his chair.

What is it? Rod?

ROD stops rocking for a moment.

ROD: Read. Read to me!

ALISON goes back to the book and starts to read again – she regularly looks up and glances at ROD during this. ROD resumes his rocking.

ALISON: 'And now, the champion, having escaped from the terrible fury of the dragon, bethinking himself of the brazen shield, and of the breaking up of the enchantment which was upon it, approached to where the shield was upon the wall; which in sooth tarried not for his full coming, but fell down at his feet upon the silver floor –'

A large wall clock falls from the wall near the nurses' station and breaks into pieces. ALISON jumps from her chair. She crosses quickly to ROD. He is still rocking back and forth as if in a trance – his eyes fixed on the door before him. ALISON places a hand on his shoulder. He shudders and smiles contortedly. ROD mumbles something to her. We hear strange echoing noises from off – snatches of songs, distortions of songs.

What? Rod, what is it? Rod!

ROD: Listen!

ALISON: What?

ROD: Can you hear it? Can you hear it? Yes, I can hear it, and I've heard it before. Long–long–long–many times, over many minutes, many hours, days, years, I've heard it–but I didn't dare…

ALISON: Rod, you're scaring me.

ROD: Pity me, miserable bastard wretch that I am! I didn't dare. I didn't dare say it. Do you know what we've done? Do you know?

ALISON: I don't know what you're talking about.

ROD: We put her in the mortuary. We shut her in there, and she was still alive.

ALISON: No, Rod –

ROD: I heard her. When we were leaving. She was scratching at the metal. But I didn't say anything. I thought I must be imagining it. But, just now – Ethelred! Ha-ha! Ha-ha-ha-ha-ha! Breaking down the hermit's door, and the death-cry of the dragon, and the shield falling on the floor –

ALISON: Rod, it's all right, it's just a story –

ROD: She was clawing her way out of that thing we shut her in. Kicking her way out. Kicking and fighting and pulling and scratching at that big steel door. Hammering at it with her fists, ripping at the copper in that doorway, until her fingers bled…and… We put her in there! She wasn't dead!

ALISON: Stop it!

ROD: She's coming to get me. Where can I go? She'll be here any minute. She's coming to get me for wanting rid of her, but I didn't. We shut her in there too quick –

ALISON: No, Rod –

ROD: I can hear her. Listen! I can hear her footsteps. Outside! Listen! I can hear her heart! Beating. Thumping! Thud! Thud! Thud! The heavy and horrible beating of her heart! Madman!

ROD jumps to his feet.

ALISON: Rod!

ROD: She's out there! I'm telling you! She's standing outside that door!

The set cracks open, revealing MADDIE standing outside. Rain is falling. MADDIE's hands and clothes are smeared with blood. She stands before them, trembling, moaning. She falls into the arms of her brother. He collapses with her – a corpse in his arms. He shudders and cries out. Then everything is still.

ALISON: Rod... Rod...

ALISON leans in to look more closely. ROD is lying dead beneath the corpse of his twin sister.

A sudden flash of light, the set cracks further open – the image of ALISON's brother, Steven, appears momentarily, then disappears. ALISON is terrified. A loud crash. Lights flicker. ALISON'S MUM appears. ALISON'S DAD appears. The MAN who climbed down to get ALISON appears. The POLICEMAN appears. Part of the fractured set rises, another part falls. The walls collapse. A flash of lightning. Thunder. The image of ALISON's brother is there again – momentarily. Then it is gone. It is as if ALISON is now standing on the rocks where she lost her brother. The wind blows hard. We hear waves crashing, water rushing, rain lashing. Another violent clap of thunder. Lightning. Another flash of the image of ALISON's brother. We hear voices echoing again:

ALISON'S VOICE: Steven! Steven!

MAN'S VOICE: Are you down there?

ALISON'S VOICE: Steven!

MUM'S VOICE: Alison!

MAN'S VOICE: Where are you?

POLICEMAN'S VOICE: What's your name?

DAD'S VOICE: Where's Stevie?

MUM'S VOICE: Alison!

MAN'S VOICE: Are you down there?

POLICEMAN'S VOICE: Can I have your autograph?

MAN'S VOICE: Are you down there?

ALISON'S VOICE: Steven!

MUM'S VOICE: Alison!

DAD'S VOICE: Where's Stevie?

A crescendo of voices and images. Then, suddenly, silence, and the stage is plunged into darkness. The sound of rain.

In the darkness we hear the opening harmony from Clear White Light, Part 2.

MADDIE (& COMPANY):
DO YOU BELIEVE
THE CLEAR WHITE LIGHT
IS GOING TO GUIDE US ON?

A blinding flash of white light, then...

SCENE 6

Thunder. The sound of the rain stops. Blood-red light up on ALISON –
sitting cross-legged on the floor, clutching the copy of the Edgar Allan
Poe book, soaked from the rain, hugging herself – mumbling quietly to
herself…

ALISON: *(From the closing paragraph of 'The Fall of the House*
of Usher.') '… Suddenly there shot along the path a wild
light, and I turned to see whence a gleam so unusual could
have issued; for the vast house and its shadows were alone
behind me. The radiance was that of the full, setting, and
blood-red moon, which now shone vividly…'

A nurse enters – it is MADDIE. ALISON continues to recite.

ALISON: '…through that
once barely-discernible
fissure. And while
I gazed, this fissure
rapidly widened and
the entire orb of the
satellite burst upon my
sight. My brain reeled as
I saw the mighty walls
rushing asunder. There
was a long tumultuous
shouting like the voice
of a thousand waters and
the deep and dank tarn
at my feet closed sullenly
and silently over the
fragments of the House
of Usher…'

ALISON: You're dead.

MADDIE: No, pet.

MADDIE: Ali! There you
are! What are you doing
out here? You're soaked.
Honestly! Come on, let's
get you inside. Ali…

MADDIE tries to lift ALISON,
but she is resistant.

Ali, come on, pet…

ROD enters.

ROD: There you are! Ali…
Ali…

MADDIE: She won't budge.

I'm Maddie. I'm your
nurse.

77

ALISON: I thought my pain killed you.

MADDIE: No. Look. I'm fine…

ROD: We're all fine.

ALISON: We put you in the mortuary.

MADDIE: No, Ali. It wasn't me.

ALISON: I didn't kill you?

MADDIE: No, pet.

ROD: It wasn't her, Ali.

MADDIE: You've not been well these past few weeks.

ROD: Come on.

ALISON: Is he here?

ROD: Who?

ALISON: Steven.

ROD: No.

MADDIE: It's just us.

ALISON: I killed my brother.

ROD: You didn't kill anyone.

MADDIE: It wasn't your fault.

ROD: Here…

> *ROD helps ALISON to her feet.*

> That's it…

MADDIE: Let me take your book…

> *ALISON hands MADDIE her book.*

ROD: Rain's clearing. And look, if I'm not very much mistaken, it's that thing people call the sun. All hail the sun!

MADDIE: I didn't know you were a sun worshipper. Did you, Ali?

ALISON: No.

MADDIE: *(Looking up.)* Would you look at that sky…

They all look up at the sky.

ALISON: It's beautiful.

MADDIE: It is.

ROD: It's what they call a mackerel sky.

MADDIE: A what?

ROD: When the clouds are all kind of rippled like that, like the pattern on a mackerel's back.

ALISON: It's lovely.

ROD: Quite magical really.

MADDIE: I love nature.

ALISON: So do I.

MADDIE: I like going for long rambles in the countryside, me.

ALISON: Can I come with you one day?

MADDIE: Course you can.

ROD: Shall we go back in?

MADDIE: Hey, maybe we can have a sing-song around the piano later? Would you like that?

ALISON: Yes.

MADDIE: Come on, then

They turn to go. ALISON stops.

Ali? Are you all right?

Beat.

ALISON: Thank you.

ROD: For what?

ALISON: I don't know. Just… Thank you.

ROD: Come on.

They exit.

Into a repeat of the a cappella opening of 'Clear White Light Part 2'…

SONG 11

Lights up on MADDIE (and company).

CLEAR WHITE LIGHT PT. 2

MADDIE (& COMPANY, WITHOUT ALISON):
DO YOU BELIEVE
THE CLEAR WHITE LIGHT
IS GOING TO GUIDE US ON?

*Drums play under as ALISON enters, wearing the long, winter coat
she wore at the start of the play.*

ALISON: That night shift was… It was like a complete loss
of control. It took over. And it was super realistic. The
things I saw. The things I heard. The things that happened.
Something cracked. And it hurt. It really hurt. Your mind
tells you something is happening, and you believe it. You
react to it. I was in hospital for about a month. It's taken a
long time to work through it. But I'm getting there. It was
just over three years ago, now. I've finished my training.
I'm about to start my new job as a nurse working in
bereavement care. I don't try to hide my scars anymore. My
scars are the story of where I've been. They're not the story
of where I'm going…

MADDIE:
RUNNING ALONG THE GROUND SINGING A
SONG IN THE MORNING LIGHT
FOLLOW FLOWERY FIELDS AS FAR AS OUT OF
SIGHT
TURNING YOUR HEAD TO THE CLOUDS AND
THE SKIES AND THE TREES
'CAUSE YOU NEVER KNOW WHAT YOU MIGHT
SEE

MADDIE & COMPANY:
DO YOU BELIEVE
THE CLEAR WHITE LIGHT
IS GOING TO GUIDE US ON
THE WAY?
SEEING THE SUN AS IT WANTS TO BE SEEN BY
EVERYONE
MELTING THE SKY THROW A HOLE IN YOUR
EYE WHERE THE MAGIC COMES
TURNING YOUR HEADS TO THE SKIES WITH
THE CLOUDS IN YOUR EYES
'CAUSE YOU NEVER KNOW WHAT YOU MIGHT
FIND

DO YOU BELIEVE
THE CLEAR WHITE LIGHT
IS GOING TO GUIDE US ON
THE WAY?

NOW IS THE TIME TO BE LOVING AND KIND TO
YOUR FELLOW MEN
SEEING THE SYMPATHY STARTING OUT ALL
OVER AGAIN
NOW IS THE TIME TO GIVE LOVE JUST ONE
MORE GO
'CAUSE YOU NEVER KNOW WHAT YOU MIGHT
KNOW

AND I BELIEVE
THE CLEAR WHITE LIGHT
IS GOING TO GUIDE US ON

YES I BELIEVE
THE CLEAR WHITE LIGHT
IS GOING TO GUIDE US ON

Lights down.

END OF PLAY

Ten Tranwellians

The cast and creative team of *Clear White Light* met staff and students at the Recovery College Collective, an education and support service for people who have used mental health services. Zoe Robinson shared the following honest and inspiring poems she had written whilst a resident patient at The Tranwell psychiatric unit at the Queen Elizabeth Hospital, Gateshead.

S

I looked into her pools of blackness:
No flame of hope could I find.
And ECT could not jolt the
Illness feeding on her mind.
Yet her soul was not empty;
She still chose words that were kind.

G

She cooked us all a Chinese dinner
Prepared with her wok from home,
Brought in by her loving husband;
Her melting spaniel eyes shone.
No time for teeth when the cops
Cruelly put the handcuffs on.

A

She saw Our Lady in her kitchen
For ten years without reprieve.
Now, each day, she calls a taxi,
Packs her bags and tries to leave.
Doctors talk of delusions;
Her one fault is to believe.

K

I didn't want to interrupt her
Voices from another land,
Yet she coped both with my questions
And their toddler-like demands.
She, when I tried to listen,
Warmly, snugly, pressed my hands.

D

She was successfully dried out but
Then she overdosed on pills:
(Gentle soul and graceful figure)
Lack of self-esteem, not thrills.
No hugs from her shamed husband,
Just disgust – a look that kills.

L

We hear her shouting in the courtyard,
Swearing, baying for a fight:
Her kids have been taken from her,
Now she's asking for a light.
Yet she still needs to nurture:
Makes us cups of tea at night.

T

She made requests in mumbled murmurs,
Trembling, trembling, head bent down:
I spread jam and dialled her numbers,
Called her troubled child in town.
Frenzied, she fights her section;
Watch her now in violence drown.

S

And a voluntary admission
Neither young nor old in years
Is the mute, frantic knitter who
Drops stitches instead of tears,
Wildly ripping up her work
As her day of discharge nears.

P

She lay there dozing on the sofa,
An empty husk for a brain:
Her son, when he came to visit,
Saw of her soul not one grain.
Her advice to us knitters:
Cut the thread and start again.

Z

Amongst the other frightened children
In this ward that broke my fall
Smiling, I try to untangle
Gently my life's woollen ball.
My way out of the illness:
To take on the writer's shawl.

Zoe Robinson

More information on Recovery College Collective:
http://www.recoverycoco.com/

By the same author

Sirett: Three Plays
A Night in Tunisia / Jamaica House / Skaville
9781840022322

Sirett: Plays Two
Worlds Apart / Crusade / This Other Eden / International Café
9781840024821

Bad Blood Blues
9781840029277

Running the Silk Road
9781840028577

Lush Life
9781840025613

The Big Life
with music by Paul Joseph
9781840024418

Rat Pack Confidential
after Shaun Levy
9781840023411

Reasons to be Cheerful
in Reasons to be Graeae: A Work in Progress
9781786823946

WWW.OBERONBOOKS.COM

Follow us on Twitter @oberonbooks
& Facebook @OberonBooksLondon